Praise for *The Only Little Prayer You Need*

"A delightful little book on healing our fear-based thoughts through prayer."

—JON MUNDY, PHD, author of
*Living A Course in Miracles*
and publisher of *Miracles* magazine

"Suppose there is a path to a better life that is really the most simple thing, the most direct route to immediate effects? And what if this cost you nothing, took little of your time, and had absolutely no risk of backfiring or hurting anybody else? You are about to find such a gift in this book, and you will soon discover that all of your fears grew out of nothing. In so doing you are also about to embark on a life where forgiveness becomes a tangible practice, and being fixated on fear becomes a thing of the past."

—DR. LEE JAMPOLSKY, author of
*Smile for No Good Reason* and
*How to Say Yes When Your Body Says No*

"Debra Engle's *The Only Little Prayer You Need* took my breath away as I sat reading it. Like Engle, I, too, have been a student of *A Course in Miracles* for thirty years. And also like her, it has taught me all the important spiritual tools I rely on every day. However, her little prayer provides a much-needed shortcut to peace-filled living that everyone, Course student or not, can use daily. Hourly, even minute by minute. Thank you, Debra. I needed to read your book today. I needed to shift my perception on a current situation and your book and prayer did just that for me."

—KAREN CASEY, PHD, author of
*Each Day a New Beginning*

# The Only Little Prayer You Need

# The Only Little Prayer You Need

The Shortest Route to a Life of Joy,
Abundance, and Peace of Mind

## Debra Landwehr Engle

HAMPTON ROADS

Copyright © 2014 by Debra Landwehr Engle
Blessing © 2014 Tenzin Gyatso, His Holiness the XIV Dalai Lama
All rights reserved. No part of this publication may be reproduced or transmitted
in any form or by any means, electronic or mechanical, including photocopying,
recording, or by any information storage and retrieval system, without
permission in writing from Red Wheel/Weiser, LLC. Reviewers may quote brief
passages.

Cover design by Jim Warner
Interior by Kathryn Sky-Peck
Typeset in Truesdell

Hampton Roads Publishing Company, Inc.
Charlottesville, VA 22906
Distributed by Red Wheel/Weiser, LLC
www.redwheelweiser.com

Sign up for our newsletter and special offers by going to
www.redwheelweiser.com/newsletter/.

ISBN: 978-1-57174-718-1

Library of Congress Cataloging-in-Publication Data available upon request.

Printed in the United States of America
MG

10  9

# Contents

# Blessing from His Holiness, the Dalai Lama

Honest concern for others is the key factor in improving our day-to-day lives. When you are warm-hearted, there is no room for anger, jealousy, or insecurity. A calm mind and self-confidence are the basis for happy and peaceful relations with each other. Healthy, happy families and a healthy, peaceful nation are dependent on warm-heartedness. Some scientists have observed that constant anger and fear eat away at our immune system, whereas a calm mind strengthens it.

We have to see how we can fundamentally change our education system so that we can train people to develop warm-heartedness early on in order to create a healthier society. I don't mean we need to change the whole system—just improve it. We need to encourage an understanding that inner peace comes from relying on human values like love, compassion, tolerance, and honesty, and that peace in the world relies on individuals finding inner peace.

—His Holiness, the Dalai Lama

# Preface

I'm not the type of person who typically asks someone to pray. That's always seemed preachy, personal, and presumptuous. In fact, I've even bristled slightly at the word "prayer"—along with "God," "Jesus," and the "Holy Spirit"—because those words have such particular meanings to each individual, and my understanding might be very different from my neighbor's.

But about thirty years ago, I started studying *A Course in Miracles*, which is described as "spiritual psychotherapy." While this course includes Christian language, it's a path not to religion, but to peace of mind—a deep peace that resides inside each of us with help from a higher power.

Even though I've studied and taught the *Course* for years, I still learn more about its teachings every day—and sometimes not in the most comfortable ways. Following any spiritual path typically is like a maze. As we make forward progress, we're likely to take a lot of detours along the way. We don't get all the answers at once. And even when we do have an "ah-ha" moment, we may find ourselves in a new and tricky part of the maze that we've never seen before.

We're at a time on this planet when we need to make a leap forward, skipping over years of wandering so we can move more directly toward peace—both within ourselves and within our world.

And that's why I'm writing this book. This story is about a seemingly small event in my life that took on miraculous significance because of the lessons that came with it.

I'm not a theologian; in fact, I've found most of my spiritual sustenance outside traditional religion. But I believe we're returning to a time when we "remember" and understand our individual connection to the divine. Each of us has a direct relationship with a higher power, and it's by calling on and developing that relationship that we can experience what might be called miraculous changes in our lives.

My husband, Bob, and I have had our share of tragedies and hurts in our lives. Both of us have gone through divorce. Bob lost his elder son to an illness no one could ever identify. We've both known times of financial struggle. And, in my capacity as co-founder of a spirituality and personal growth program, I've worked for years with women who are experiencing everything from the lifelong effects of early sexual abuse to the uncertainty of their primary relationship, their stage of life, or their children's futures due to mental health or drug abuse issues.

The way we deal with all of these challenges defines the quality of our life and our peace of mind. And with the help of the *Course*, I also know that trying to do it without help from a higher power is not going to get us where we want to go.

I believe that when you use the prayer in this book, you'll experience steady progress toward a life of greater internal peace. Much of the drama and chaos around you will subside. And what remains will have less impact on you, bouncing off of you because you're no longer a willing host.

As crazy as it sounds, I think this prayer is an *answer* to prayer. It's a path to a better life. And it's the simplest thing possible. Now all we have to do is actually use it.

So here I am, asking you to pray.

*one*

# The Prayer

It was January 11, 2013, and I felt like it had already been a long year. Earlier in the week, I'd made a significant mistake with a major client. And, even though everyone on my project team was gracious and understanding, I had a hard time forgiving myself for it. In fact, at three o'clock the next morning, I woke up panicked that I'd sent the wrong file to the same client. I felt like someone had shoved a lit torch down my throat.

Tired, and clearly not in the best of moods, I drove with my husband, Bob, to pick up our Honda CR-V at the body shop. The driver's door had been damaged in a minor accident at a grocery store parking lot. After renting a series of cars, I was ready to climb into a vehicle that fit me again.

When I did, I was pleased to see that the dent was repaired, as was the gap between the window and the doorframe. Bob opened my driver's door to check it out.

"It looks good," I said. "I'm happy."

But the door didn't close properly. Bob opened it and shut it harder, but he had to slam it before it latched. My mood, which had been momentarily lifted, started again on a downward slope.

Bob talked to the body shop manager and made arrangements for more repair in the next couple of weeks. In the meantime, we figured, we could go ahead and return the rental.

I drove the CR-V, following Bob down the highway toward the interstate. Before long, I heard a rattle in the dash, then a vibration. Every time I hit a bump in the road, it seemed like the rattles got worse—and so did my attitude.

*It's not really fixed*, I thought. *It has to go back to the shop, and it'll never be right.* From there, my thoughts took a nosedive. I thought about the fact that the accident had been preventable. *It wouldn't have happened if I'd been driving instead of Bob.* My thoughts headed fast into a cesspool, all blaming Bob, the body shop mechanic, or myself for weeks of inconvenience, expense and frustration. As I drove, I become more miserable.

I don't know about you, but I've spent *way* too much time in that cesspool during my life. Despite the fact that I've long been a student of spiritual traditions, meditation, and spiritual practices—I've even taught them for many years—I still find my thoughts drifting too much to the negative. I can easily fall into irritation or frustration. When I'm stressed, I'm unkind and snippy, sometimes downright mean.

As we arrived at the car dealership to return the rental, I was exhausted. Not just from the last few minutes of negative thinking, but from years of it. In this case, I was afraid the CR-V would never be right. I was afraid I'd never forgive Bob. I was afraid I'd always be mad that he was driving the day of the accident. I was afraid we wouldn't get reimbursed from the insurance company. I was afraid, as I've been many times before, that I would continue to be unhappy.

I had had all these thoughts, or some facsimile of them, literally hundreds if not thousands of times before. Our issues of money, unexpected events and the future were never resolved. It wasn't because Bob and I never talked about them; we did. But somehow nothing ever really seemed to shift.

As I sat in the CR-V while Bob went inside to handle the paperwork, I genuinely wanted to do something different, but that was just it: *I* couldn't do it. My mind had created the problem, and I couldn't fix it with that same mind. What I wanted was a breath of fresh air—a *whoosh* of love, acceptance, and healing. I knew that couldn't come from me. It had to come from another power.

I thought about my options, and the only one that seemed feasible was to ask for help. I sat back in the driver's seat, looked out over the sea of cars at the dealership parking lot, and found myself saying these words to the Holy Spirit:

*Please*

# heal

*my*

*fear-based*

T H O U G H T S .

I had never said that prayer before. In fact, it just showed up. And at the time, it didn't seem like anything remarkable. After all, when we're in pain, we turn to a higher power for healing with whatever words come from the heart. But what happened next took it to a whole different level.

*two*

# What It Means

When Bob got in the CR-V, I was still in a bad mood. The prayer hadn't changed anything—or so I thought.

"Well," I began, with plenty of attitude, "there are big rattles in the dash, and one time I heard wind coming through the driver's window."

Bob jotted down notes for the body shop manager. "Anything else?" he asked, genuinely helpful.

"No," I said glumly as I pulled out into traffic. "You'll hear the rattles when we hit some bumps."

I pulled onto the interstate, and Bob trained his ear toward the dashboard to hear what I was talking about. We hit a couple of bumps and . . . nothing. No rattle, no vibration. I figured the vibrations were muffled by the road noise in heavy traffic. But we hit more bumps . . . still nothing.

About halfway home, Bob said, "I haven't heard anything yet, have you?"

"No," I said, almost disappointed. How could I make him feel guilty if nothing was wrong? "We'll hear it when we get on the highway," I said, thinking bigger bumps would reveal the rattles.

But there weren't any. Not a single sound all the way home. The problems seemed to have disappeared.

*Huh*, I thought, still pouting as we pulled in the drive.

When I went inside, part of me was glad, and another part felt cheated. I'd wanted to punish Bob by saying, "See, it's really messed up and it's all your fault."

I hung up my coat, looked through the mail, and then started hearing my inner voice talking. Essentially, this is what it said:

> *When you asked for your thoughts to be healed, the external triggers for those thoughts were no longer needed, and so the rattles went away.*

*Oh*, I thought, in the mundane sort of way that sometimes precedes great change. A change in my *internal* perception had just shifted my *external* environment. This, in the teachings of *A Course in Miracles*, would qualify as a miracle, a return to what the *Course* calls "right-mindedness."

As long as I was rattled, I needed rattles in my dash to help me heal. But when my thoughts were healed, the rattles were no longer needed.

This "ah-ha" moment spread through me slowly like a warm drink. I realized it was big—something that, despite all my years of spiritual study, I had never understood in quite this way before.

Wayne Dyer has long said: "Change the way you look at things, and the things you look at change." In other words, change your perception, and your world looks different.

I get that. If I believe the world is a scary place, I'm going to see dangerous situations everywhere. If I change my perception to believing the world is a safe place, I'm going to see help and support everywhere.

But this was different.

"Change the way
you look at things,
and the things
you look at
change."

—Wayne Dyer

"Bob," I said, "we have something important to talk about, and it's really good, so let's sit down." I'm sure he could detect a change of tone in my voice.

We sat at the kitchen counter, opened a bag of Ruffles and a bag of carrots, and propped our legs on each other's chairs like we usually do.

I explained the whole trip to the rental car facility and how angry I had been. I told him how I asked for my fear-based thoughts to be healed—after which the rattles in the car had disappeared.

"I think this is what happened," I said. "We come into this life with certain lessons to learn about love and acceptance. And so every situation and relationship is here to help us become more loving and accepting. They give us opportunities to learn.

"When we ask for our fear-based thoughts to be healed, we're asking to replace fear with love and acceptance. When our thoughts are healed, we no longer need the lesson, and the circumstances or issues go away."

It struck me that this truly is the secret. *When our thoughts are healed, we no longer need the lesson, and the circumstances or issues go away*. It's also incredibly simple, which is why we struggle against it or forget to ask for help. How could it possibly be effective when it's so easy? But when we can remember to ask for our thoughts to be healed, not only are *we* changed, our "problems" may eventually cease to exist.

After munching on a few more potato chips and carrots, Bob and I pulled out a sheet of paper and wrote down all the major things we have fear thoughts about. Money: earning, spending, saving, and investing. Our home and property. Our businesses. Friends and family. Hormones. The economy. As the list grew, we realized we have fear-based thoughts about pretty much everything in one way or another.

Then, for the next thirty minutes, we went through each item on the list, taking turns asking that our fear-based thoughts about that item be healed so we could be restored to right-mindedness.

In some cases our requests were generic; in some cases they were more specific. With health, Bob asked for his fear-based thoughts about glaucoma and his gluten intolerance to be healed. For money, I asked for my fears about retirement savings to be healed.

We went through the entire list, taking our time, being thoughtful about every item. When we were done, we weren't sure what had just happened, or what would happen next. But I can tell you one thing: my bad mood was long gone, and harmony had been restored.

*three*

# What Is Fear?

The story of the CR-V may seem unremarkable, but that's really the point. In life, we often look for big stories, big miracles: the woman who lifts the bus off her child, or the blind person whose sight is suddenly restored. But the real miracle is the change in our minds that makes it possible for us to live a life of joy and peace rather than one of struggle and internal chaos. Those miracles are available to us every day, simply by shifting from fear to love. The trick is to make that shift in a real and lasting way.

That's why, after Bob and I talked, the warm drink inside me felt more nourishing as I realized how profound this was. I sat down at the computer and started to write about it. "This is BIG!" I wrote. "Really, really BIG! We don't need to fix the problem. We need to have our thoughts about the problem healed. When we do that, there's no longer a need for the lesson. Whatever needed to be fixed or healed will no longer be an issue."

At the risk of sounding overly dramatic, I believe this is the answer we're looking for. This is the one thing that could change your world.

Let me tell you why I believe that so strongly.

According to *A Course in Miracles*, our minds have two sides. One is the ego. Unlike our traditional definition of the ego, which connotes people who are boastful or full of themselves, the *Course* makes the ego seem like a two-year-old on speed. Demanding, prone to tantrums and outbursts, the ego runs on fear.

The other part represents the higher Self, which remembers that we are children of God. Quiet and respectful, it communicates through whispers and gentle nudges as it expresses and extends divine love.

We live in a world that feeds our egos with fear. We're bombarded by fear-based messages every day. Terrorism will get us, or earthquakes or global warming or the economy. And we're constantly judged or judging ourselves: for what we're wearing, our hair, our car, our home, our productivity, our performance on the job, our kids' accomplishments, and on and on. Once you start to break it down, you see that fear is pervasive, like a cancer that's gotten into our bones.

We can also feed our higher Selves in this world, but we do that in a different way—one that's not nearly as sexy as big drama can be. We feed it through meditation, self-reflection, stillness, time in nature, and other typically quiet pursuits that allow us to listen to the voice within. By doing these things, we become more aware of the light within us, the love that is the essence of who we are.

Think of it this way: Our essence, or love, is like a flame that never goes out. But that flame burns inside a lantern that's covered in dirt—covered in fear. The more fearful our thoughts, the more opaque the walls of the lantern become, until we can't see the flame inside at all. We may forget the flame is there, or feel like it has no impact on our lives because we don't know how to access it. At that point, fear rules our existence.

That's why the *Course* says, "Your task is not to seek for love, but merely to seek and find all of the barriers within yourself that you have built against it." In other words, while the world piles fear on top of our light, our job is to remember that light within. When we do, whatever seemed to conceal it ceases to exist.

That's where the prayer comes in.

*Please*

# heal

*my*

*fear-based*

THOUGHTS.

Let's look more closely at fear and love. When I teach the *Course*, I find it helps to picture two trees. Let's name one the "Fear Tree" and the other the "Love Tree."

I do this is because our typical definitions of *fear* and *love* are limited. When we think of fear, we usually think of things we're afraid of: cancer, economic crisis, losing our jobs, our kids being hurt, personal loss, death.

When we think of love, we typically think of romantic love, or the love we have for our kids, or our pets, or our best friend.

But when you stop to really think about it, all our emotions are rooted in either the Fear Tree or the Love Tree.

The branches of the Love Tree yield kindness, compassion, caring, creativity, joy, playfulness, peace, acceptance, and the biggest one, forgiveness—all the feelings that are rooted in love.

The branches of the Fear Tree yield hurt, anger, meanness, violence, and the biggest one, judgment—all the feelings that are rooted in fear.

"A lot of the thoughts we think every day—the overwhelming majority of them—are rooted in fear."

In fact, fear yields many things that we don't usually attribute to it. It may be easy, for instance, to see how worry is rooted in fear. But how is, say, boastfulness a form of fear? Well, let's trace it back to where it comes from: you feel insecure about your worth, you feel you've got to prove yourself, and so you brag about your accomplishments. In truth, you're afraid that people won't like you, that you don't matter, that you don't deserve to be here. When you're boastful, you're really acting from fear.

A lot of the thoughts we think every day—and I mean the overwhelming majority of them—are rooted in fear. And yet we don't think about them that way because they're about the mundane, like rattles in the dashboard. Sure, we're aware of major threats: job loss, death, life-changing illness, financial collapse, natural disasters, terrorist attacks. But the insidiousness of fear is that it creeps into the cracks *between* those threats and settles in, often unnoticed. It becomes a constant cover of darkness that never allows us to fully experience the inner light.

Let's look at a list of fear-based thoughts as a quick reference.

- Abandonment

- Anger

- Anxiety

- Attack

- Boastfulness

- Bullying

- Control

- Conformity, living according to others' expectations at the expense of your unique gifts

- Depression

- False humility

- Feeling superior to others

- Feeling not good enough, unloved, as though you don't matter

- Gossip

- Greed

- Grief

- Guilt
- Insecurity
- Irritation
- Jealousy
- Judgment
- Loneliness
- Malevolence
- Martyrdom
- Meanness
- Need for power
- Nervousness
- Panic
- Pessimism
- Poverty
- Revenge
- Sacrifice
- Sadness

- Scarcity
- Shame
- Suspicion
- Distrust
- Unhappiness
- Violence

This is not a complete list. And I'm not saying these emotions are all "bad." They're part of our human experience. Grief, for instance, can be an expression of love, and it's an important part of healing. Anger can produce great clarity.

The goal is not to eradicate fear thoughts or emotions, but to shift from thought practices that are primarily fear-based to ones that are primarily love-based. Let's look at a list of love-based thoughts:

Compassion
Willingness
Respect
Creativity
Generosity
Acceptance
Confidence
Expansion
Contentedness
Forgiveness
Confidence
Presence
Healing
Caring
Gifts
Sharing
Patience
Kindness
Gratitude
Forgiveness
Encouragement
Solace
Joy
Grace
Patience
Healing
Caring
Comfort
Honesty
Respect
Comfort
Kindness
Presence
Gratitude
Solace
Generosity
Willingness
Delight
Forgiveness
Honesty
Peace
Freedom
Comfort
Playfulness
Courtesy

- Acceptance
- Caring
- Comfort
- Compassion
- Confidence
- Contentedness
- Courtesy
- Creativity
- Delight
- Encouragement
- Expansion
- Forgiveness
- Freedom
- Generosity
- Gifts

- Grace

- Gratitude

- Healing

- Honesty

- Joy

- Kindness

- Patience

- Peace

- Playfulness

- Presence

- Respect

- Sharing

- Solace

- Warm-heartedness

- Willingness

One more thing: I mentioned that judgment is the biggest nut on the Fear Tree. Why? Because it makes us think we're separate from others—especially separate from God. Think of everything that judgment can lead to: bullying, violence, resentment, lack of forgiveness, loneliness. In each case, judgment leads to isolation and an "us vs. them" mentality. Here's the simplest of examples:

I see an old classmate and think, *Boy, she looks old. She must have put on thirty pounds. And why doesn't she color her hair? It would make her look so much younger.*

First of all, *ick*. But these are the kinds of thoughts that can pop into our minds, right? Really, though, how is this an example of fear? And, besides the fact that these thoughts are rude, they are just *unspoken* thoughts, so what's the harm?

Any time we're judging someone else, it's our ego trying to make itself feel better by comparing and coming out on top. And that means we're afraid we're not good enough, so we have to trounce somebody else.

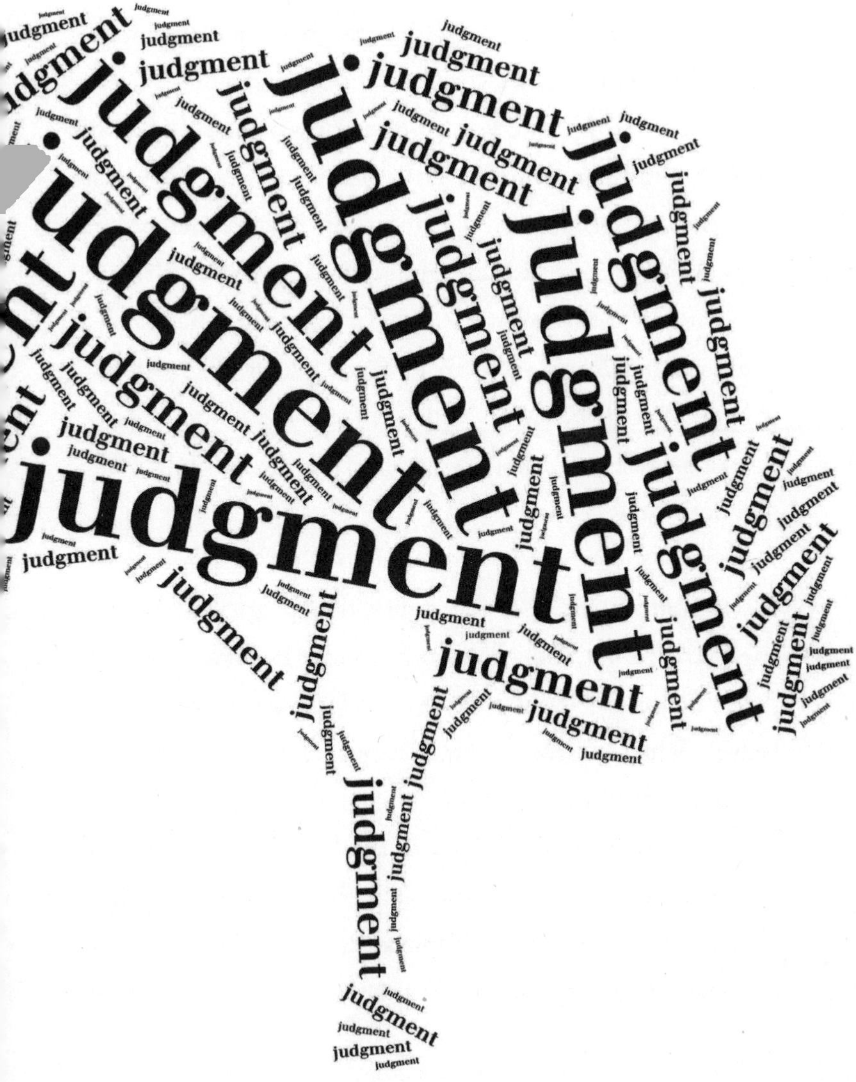
judgment

Of course, we know this doesn't work. Not only does it *not* make you feel better to judge someone, it actually makes you feel worse. It makes you feel separate and alone. So you become more disconnected from your essence as a child of God, diminishing yourself a little more. You heap more fear onto the light inside you. You smear a little more mud on the sides of the lantern, and the light seems dimmer yet.

This is what we all know, right? This is the Golden Rule. Every religion has a form of it. Some people might honor it because they believe it will earn their way into heaven. But right here and now, it's good mental health. Important psychotherapy.

Think about it. Why do people go to therapists? Because they feel depressed, they feel guilty, they're grieving, they're angry, they don't know how to find peace in themselves and their relationships. Most aren't trying to earn their way into heaven. They're trying to experience contentment and peace of mind right now, every day.

What we're talking about is the key to living with the peace of God *while you're here*. You can live in hell (fear) or heaven (love). The prayer reminds us that, every minute of every day, we can make a better choice.

"Every minute of

every day,

we can

make a better

choice."

Here are a few things you might experience as a result of the prayer's healing.

- Being less irritable
- Being more patient
- Laughing more
- Being more considerate
- Feeling you have more time
- Relaxing more easily
- Having more energy
- Feeling more harmony in your home
- Respecting yourself and others more
- Valuing yourself more
- Letting go of resentments and blame
- Worrying less
- Putting less pressure on yourself
- Being more present with yourself and others

- Noticing serendipitous events more
- Seeing the meaning in life events
- Making decisions more easily
- Worrying less about the future
- Making things easy rather than hard
- Letting go of the need to struggle
- Feeling more hopeful
- Letting go of obligations that don't serve you
- Feeling less guilt or shame
- Caring less about what others think
- Recovering from a bad mood faster
- Feeling freer to be yourself
- Trusting yourself, others, and the world more
- Being clearer about what you want and what you don't want
- Saying no without guilt

*four*

# How Does Fear
# Impact Your Life?

One of my clients, a successful forty-something business owner, told me she doesn't believe she's ever been happy. "I have had happy days, like a vacation or day spent with someone, but there's always this cloud of discontent that covers everything. I would love to just relax and think everything's going to be okay, but I just never have been able to do that."

This is why the prayer is so important.

Fear keeps us confined to unhappiness. Years ago, I felt like I was trapped in a plastic bag. I could see out, and others could see in, but something was confining me. It was fear— fear of being myself, fear of expressing my gifts, fear of letting my light shine.

So why is fear so pervasive in our lives, and how does it take such firm control of us?

## *We're taught to be afraid from the time we're born.*

It's true that there are lots of dangers in this physical world, and fear acts as our protector. It keeps us from stepping in front of a moving vehicle, raises a red flag when we're with people who might harm us, picks out matching outfits from our closet so we'll avoid ridicule, and gets us to the doctor when we need medical attention.

But there's a difference between making smart decisions and living your whole life feeding from the Fear Tree. Unlike love, which nourishes you and supports your vitality, fear drains you of energy and diminishes the joy of living.

## *Fear-based thoughts perpetuate an illusion.*

*A Course in Miracles* says that, in this world, there's love, and there's fear. Of those two, only love is real, while fear is an illusion. This can be a difficult concept to grasp unless you look at it this way: if you trace any fear-based thought to its roots, you'll find the same core fear: *I don't matter*. But since we are *all* children of God, this simply cannot be true. You cannot be an extension of God and not have value; it's not possible. So all fear-based thoughts grow out of nothing, an illusion. This is why even the deepest scars in our lives and societies can be healed quickly and completely if we'll focus on forgiveness rather than remaining fixated on fear.

## *Fear-based thoughts can be deceiving.*

Our worry about others, for instance, might seem like a natural part of being a parent or a friend. But worry is a denial of God, and that's what the ego is all about. If we truly trusted that everything is happening according to a plan we can't understand and don't need to control, we wouldn't worry. We would have peace of mind—not from denial or in a powerless way, but with spiritual strength, knowing that our job is to honor our own journey and those journeys of others.

Sometimes, worrying about others, just like worrying about ourselves, is the ego's way of saying, "See? I'm a nice person. I'm responsible. I care"—when it's really just a way of hiding the fact that we're scared. Worrying about others makes fear not just acceptable, it makes it noble. But here's the truth: caring about others is love; worrying about them is fear.

## *We are addicted to fear.*

People who are in a twelve-step program admit they have a problem and that they're powerless over it, and they turn that problem over to a higher power.

But that's just for those who have hit bottom, right?

Well, guess what? We've all hit bottom. We're all addicted, and what we're addicted to is fear. Just like the initial steps of the twelve-step program, the prayer surrenders our problems to a higher power who can perform the healing we're not able to do for ourselves.

This is the case in every situation that comes from fear, but it might be easiest to see in instances of self-sabotage. The twenty-year-old son of a friend, for instance, has spent several weeks in jail over the past year for theft and drug use. He told his mom that he wants to do better, and he doesn't understand why he keeps sabotaging himself when he knows he could make other choices.

The answer? Fear.

I know that seems strange—how could anyone be afraid of living *within* the law? Doesn't it make more sense to be afraid of going to jail? This seeming paradox illustrates the insanity of the ego. As long as you believe you're not worthy of a better life, as long as you feel guilty and beat yourself up over past transgressions, you will keep making decisions from fear. And sometimes those decisions will land you in jail.

"The prayer surrenders our problems to a higher power who can perform the healing we're not able to do for ourselves."

For my friend's son, every time he tries to make a positive change, the addictive ego will call to him. Being in jail is just a reflection of how he's imprisoned by his own thoughts. That's why he, like all of us, needs divine intervention. No matter our transgressions—from hurting a loved one to committing murder—we pile on layers of guilt, reinforcing the fear around our inner light. As *A Course in Miracles* says, we don't need God's forgiveness, because we already have that. But we do need our own, with the help of the Holy Spirit.

## *Fear-based thoughts express themselves in the body.*

We know that stress and worry contribute to physical ailments and slow the body's ability to heal. But until I started the practice of asking for my fear-based thoughts to be healed, I hadn't been aware how much my body was absorbing and living with fear.

As I've since become more aware of my thoughts and physical experience, I can now feel how often my stomach tightens when I'm nervous or how my shoulders hunch when I'm stressed. I'm now aware of how often my jaw is clenched and even my toes are curled. Now, a few times a day, I tune into my body and feel how much fear it's carrying, and I relax and ask that all my fear-based thoughts be healed.

I know the prayer is good for our mental and emotional health. I have no doubt it's good for our physical health as well.

### *A huge percentage of fear-based thoughts are in anticipation of things that never happen.*

Saying the prayer will make you acutely aware of this. By asking for your fear-based thoughts to be healed, you can be assured that whatever you were afraid of will go away. It may not happen immediately, but it will diminish over time. This is a good reminder of the fact that the job description for your life does not include the word "worry." In fact, worry in all its many forms is just another attempt by the ego to usurp control.

"The job description
for your life
does not include the
word 'worry.'"

*A huge percentage of fear-based thoughts are about minutiae, but we blow them up into big drama.*

I think we do this partly to convince ourselves that our lives have meaning. If I have problems, if I'm overly busy, if I have to deal with all this *stuff*, then I must have value. I must matter. That's what the ego tells itself. But there's a line in *A Course in Miracles* that says our ego can't accept how little we need to do. That's because we never have to prove that we deserve to be here.

We also don't have to fight our fears, although this concept threatens the ego in a big way. After all, everybody loves a hero—the college kid who was terrified of public speaking and overcame the fear to deliver a moving speech. Or the small-town girl who confronts her fear and builds a successful business in the big city. We all love that "We did it!" moment of jubilation, of slaying the dragons within ourselves and in the world around us. It's part of the human drama. Yet, while overcoming and fighting fears can build character, those approaches also make the fear real, reinforcing the idea that we're broken or insufficient at our core.

Years ago, I joined a large Rotary International club that was 95 percent male and filled with successful and influential business leaders. Every time I walked into one of the lunch meetings, I felt like I didn't belong. I wasn't wearing a suit, I didn't have political connections, and I didn't run a multimillion-dollar organization. Finally a wise person said to me, "If you want them to accept you, start by accepting them first." Ahh. I'd been so internally focused on trying to overcome my fear of fitting in that I'd missed the bigger picture: the "problem" I was trying to fix didn't exist.

When we ask for our fear-based thoughts to be healed, we see that the dramas we worry about—and perpetuate—matter much less than we realize, and that the essence of who we are matters more. We don't have to prove our existence to anyone. There's enormous peace of mind in that.

## *Our fear creates the very thing we're afraid of.*

I had an ah-ha moment years ago when I was making my bed one day, thinking about something good that had happened in my life. Immediately after that thought, I felt a wave of fear.

"When we ask for our fear-based thoughts to be healed, we see that the dramas we worry about matter much less than we realize."

When would the other shoe drop? At that moment (I'm not making this up), my inner voice said very clearly, "There is no other shoe." And at the same time, I heard a clunk in my bedroom closet. When I looked, I saw a shoe on the floor. It apparently had defied physics and thrown itself out of the shoe organizer, just to make the point.

*Okay, I get it*, I said to myself and whoever was listening. From that point on, my fear of the other shoe dropping disappeared.

The fact is, the only "shoe" out there is one you create with your own expectations. If you think something negative will befall you, you'll look for it, anticipate it, magnetize it, amplify it, and put it squarely in your line of sight. It's not a lightning bolt from a punishing God, and you're not the victim of a random universe; it's simply a belief, a piece of fruit from the Fear Tree landing with a thump on your head.

So consider that maybe you're not being punished, that there's no cosmic score sheet balancing your wins with losses. The freedom to fully enjoy all of life is available to all of us. But, like everything, first we have to be free of the beliefs that stand in our way.

## *Fear keeps you stuck.*

Fear is the reason that, instead of going out and creating our dreams, we just play around the edges—for weeks, months, even years. The ego constantly makes excuses to prevent us from moving forward: *It's not the right time. I don't have the proper equipment. I don't know enough. I don't have the right degree. I don't have enough money. It's raining.*

Typically, these excuses are all code for something much deeper: *I'm afraid I'm not good enough.* Or, conversely: *I'm afraid of my own power.* For instance, I know two people who have shown interest in Internet dating in the past couple of years. One thought about it, did her due diligence in researching the service that was right for her, signed up, and met someone within a few weeks who turned out to be an excellent match. The other has been thinking, planning, reading, talking about it—preparing for it—for more than a year. This may be exactly what he needs—time to fully process his intentions. Or, this could be stalling, his ego saying, "Let's just pretend we're ready for a relationship. We'll do everything leading up to it without actually signing up so we can convince ourselves

"When the

fear-based thought

is healed, you're free

to take steps toward

your desire

without barriers

getting in the way."

there's progress, even though we're scared about actually meeting someone, being happy, and growing."

The clue is usually when someone says, "Oh, I've been busy, so I haven't gotten to it yet." I've used that excuse for years on an assortment of projects. Busy-ness is a decoy, an accepted excuse for, "I'm too afraid to do it." When the fear-based thought is healed, you're free to experience clarity of purpose and take steps toward your desire without barriers getting in the way.

So, whatever it is—losing weight, getting regular exercise, being honest about what you want, moving into a leadership role, writing a book, starting your own business, speaking up, leaving a relationship or situation that doesn't serve you—if you keep saying, "I'm going to do it," and keep planning and preparing but never actually completing it, *you probably have fear in the way.*

## *Fear-based thoughts are seductive.*

They're like the sirens of Greek mythology—beautiful island women who sang songs of enchantment and allure. The only problem was that, when sailors steered toward those mesmerizing voices, they shipwrecked on the rocky coast.

Similarly, fear-based thoughts call to us with false promises of safety:

"Having a dream is fine, but if you follow it, you might fail. It's much safer to keep working at this dead-end job. At least you have a steady paycheck."

"Sure, some of the people in this neighborhood need help, but it's better not to get involved. You're just inviting trouble if you do."

"I'd like to get out and make some friends, but it's a lot of work to get to know people. I probably wouldn't meet anyone I like anyway."

Every time we start to sail toward joy and happiness, the ego calls us back. That's why we need divine intervention. The pull of the ego is strong, we're deeply entrenched in fear-based conditioning, and that conditioning is reinforced minute by minute. As a result, it takes extraordinary willingness, vigilance, and commitment to free ourselves from it. That's why, thank God, we have the Holy Spirit.

## *Fear from the outside breeds fear on the inside.*

Just for a day, pay attention to all the fear-based messages you hear. Those messages will astound you—everything from "You're likely to be a victim of identify theft" to "If you don't have $2 million saved for retirement by the time you're fifty, you'll spend the last few years of your life on the streets."

You'll hear alarming statistics—about getting cancer, or how unlikely you are to find a mate after forty; the odds of having a child with addiction issues, or of losing your job. And then there's the long list of symptoms (typically including death) that are side effects of drugs advertised on TV. Even conversations around the water cooler or at family get-togethers often drift toward impending economic doom or a relative's struggle with Alzheimer's. And, always, the underlying message is, "This could happen to you."

The point is—once you start to sensitize your mind to fear messages in your external world, you'll see how ingrained they are in what we read, hear, see, and discuss every day, creating a constant undercurrent of instability.

"Just for a day,

pay attention to

all the fear-based

messages you

hear."

### *Fear keeps us from experiencing life as the wondrous opportunity it is.*

It tunes us to a channel in which everything looks frightening. The past is filled with guilt, shame, and regret. The future is unknown, and could bring us anything from late-in-life poverty to ecological disaster, or both. And when we spend so much time pondering our fears from the past and for the future, we lose a clear view of the joy available in the present moment.

Fear robs us of the sweetness and gentleness of life that's possible when we have peace of mind. When we're high on fear, we could be in heaven itself and not recognize it for what it is. We'd mistake angels for the flying monkeys from *The Wizard of Oz*, and we'd worry about getting a sunburn and, ultimately, melanoma from all that bright light. I can just hear your ego as you stand at the pearly gates: "Wait," it would say, "I forgot my SPF 30!"

"When we're high

on fear, we could

be in heaven itself

and not recognize it

for what it is."

*five*

# What Makes This Prayer Different?

Here's how we usually pray:

> *Please let my team win.*

> *Please make my mom well.*

> *Please keep my children safe.*

> *Please help me get this job.*

> *Please help me win the lottery.*

In other words, we're asking for something or someone *in our external environment* to change. In contrast, think about this prayer:

*Please*

# heal

*my*

*fear-based*

THOUGHTS.

With this prayer, you're not asking for any change in the world around you. You're asking for *yourself* to be rearranged, knowing that the world around you will be rearranged as a result.

In other words, it's the exact opposite of how we usually pray.

Maybe one of your prayers goes something like this: "Please help us find the money to pay our mortgage this month." Saying the prayer may help you feel like the burden of that month's mortgage has been lifted. But your ego—the part of you that feeds on fear—will simply seek out new financial worries to keep you awake at night. *Even if we can pay it this month, what are we going to do next month? What if I lose my job and our income dries up? What if I fall and break my arm, and then we've got medical bills to pay?* The prayer gives you temporary relief, but it doesn't change anything *in you*, so your old patterns remain intact.

In contrast, asking "Please heal my fear-based thoughts about our mortgage" also gives you a sense of relief. But instead of lifting just that burden, it relieves the need to recreate that fear and hold onto it. This prayer heals your very *desire* for burdens, your addiction to fear-based thoughts, freeing you to live without that fear and with greater peace of mind. As a result, your financial situation is free to improve. That's what makes it so different.

When you ask to be in right alignment with love, everything is possible. Your life starts to shift around you. The world of form changes because it is now governed by love rather than fear. The rattles in your dashboard begin to disappear because you no longer believe that you deserve them, or that hardship is your destiny. The mud is wiped clean from the lantern, and the light shines through without anything obscuring its brightness.

This means that everything rooted in love can be fully experienced: harmony, abundance, joy, well-being, and peace of mind.

This does away with the need for struggle. The struggle is always over fixing the problem or being good enough or pretty enough or smart enough or clever enough or finding the right person or the right job. But this is simply asking

"With this prayer,
you're asking for
*yourself* to be
rearranged, knowing
that the world around
you will be rearranged
as a result."

that our thoughts about all those things be healed. When we do that, the need for the problem is removed, along with the barriers that keep us from experiencing abundance and joy in all its forms.

"Problems" or things that need to be fixed only exist as opportunities for us to learn to be more loving, accepting, and compassionate. Even our bodies are just vehicles in this life, and they provide opportunities for us to learn those things as well.

When we hold onto fear, we are paralyzed, burdened, slowed down, beaten up and abused by it, even when we don't think we're directing it at ourselves or the world around us. And without even knowing it, we perpetuate it. Our ego makes sure of that.

So, again, don't ask for something or someone to be fixed or healed. Ask for your *thoughts* to be healed so that love can take the place of fear.

"The cause of your fear is in your mind, not in the external world. So when you heal that cause, the effect is to change the external world."

Instead of asking for your marriage to be healed, ask for your fear-based thoughts about the marriage and your spouse to be healed.

Instead of asking for your money

situation to be healed,

ask for your fear-based

thoughts about money

to be healed.

Instead of asking for your body to be healed, ask for your fear-based thoughts about your body to be healed.

Instead of asking to get home safely, ask for your fear-based thoughts about the journey to be healed.

Instead of asking that you get an

"A" on the test, ask for your

fear-based thoughts about

studying and success

to be healed.

Instead of asking for your baby to

be healthy, ask for your

fear-based thoughts about

your baby's health

to be healed.

Do you see how this works? One is asking for the external world to change to make you happy and feel safe. The other is asking that your thoughts be healed. *And as a result, the external world will change.*

The cause of your fear is in your mind, not in the external world. So when you heal that cause, the effect is to change the external world.

The thing that's so exciting about this prayer is that it works on every level.

I know this might sound Pollyannaish, naïve, simplistic, idealistic—or just plain strange to some people.

That's why I know it works.

Our society believes in fear. So when you present an idea that resolves fear—in fact dissolves it, and not of our own doing—it's going to sound impossible. Wishful thinking, some might call it.

Here's what one woman had to say after using the prayer:

*The first time I used it, all of a sudden, the fear was gone. I thought, wow, that was simple. It just went away.*

*As I kept doing it, I noticed it created a space . . . allowed me to have better understanding of what the fear might be, and maybe a cause or two. In that space, I didn't feel the fear. Everything seemed clear for just a little bit.*

*After doing this for two or three weeks, the next time a fear came up, it didn't run away with me—or I didn't run away with it—because I'd experienced this relief and this space and it wasn't one specific fear, it had a general healing effect.*

If that's wishful thinking, I have just one thing to say: Let the wishing begin.

# six

# How Do You Say the Prayer?

The prayer is simple, but there's a lot to it, so let's break it down.

## Who are you praying to?

This may seem like a silly question. Don't prayers go to God? Or Jesus, Mother Mary, the Creator, Yahweh, Jehovah, Divine Intelligence, Source, or another higher power?

I would answer that question with a resounding yes. I'm not one to split hairs when it comes to spirituality. To me, your beliefs (or lack of them) are a personal and sacred matter, and I trust that you'll address this prayer to the entity or energy that's right for you. In fact, I even know agnostics and atheists who embrace the prayer (although they wouldn't call it that), because they acknowledge its psychological value in a world where fear-based thinking is rampant.

Having said that, I'll also tell you why, when I use the prayer, I specifically ask the Holy Spirit to be on the receiving end. *A Course in Miracles* says the Holy Spirit is the communicator between us and God. The *Course*, in fact, describes the Holy Spirit in countless ways. It says He teaches us the difference between pain and joy. "He brings

the light of truth into the darkness and lets it shine on you."
And the *Course* says the Holy Spirit "seems to be a Voice,
for in that form He speaks God's Word to you. He seems
to be a Guide through a far country, for you need that form
of help."

It also says that vengeance—or any other form of fear—
cannot be shared, because it creates division and separation.
"Give it therefore to the Holy Spirit," the *Course* says, "who
will undo it in you because it does not belong in your mind,
which is part of God."

This is why I pray to the Holy Spirit. At the same time, I
have no fear that our prayers are heard, no matter what name
we invoke. When prayers come from loving hearts, certainly
the heart of love receives them.

## Is the specific wording important?

I don't often say you have to do something a certain way,
especially when it comes to spirituality, but I do think the
words make a difference, and I'd advise you to say it this way:

*Please*

# heal

*my*

*fear-based*

THOUGHTS.

Here's why:

After the CR-V day, I started using the prayer whenever fear-based thoughts came up (which meant ALL the time). I found myself saying, "Please *help me* let go of my fears about . . ." or, "Please *let me release* my fear-based thoughts about . . ."

These word choices may seem minor, but they're not. If I'm asking the Holy Spirit to *help me* let go of my fears or release my fear-based thoughts, then I'm asking for *me* to be part of the solution. And the fact is, I can't be. I can't solve the problem with the same mind that created it. It's simply the two-year-old ego trying to assert itself again.

Our human experience is a story in which there are heroes and villains, love is unrequited and people hold beliefs like "no pain, no gain." We see countless versions of that story modeled over and over again until the drama seems natural and unavoidable. So it's no surprise that fears move into our minds and settle in for the long haul, putting their feet up on the couch, helping themselves to anything in the refrigerator, and refusing to pick up after themselves. As infuriating as they are, they've become so familiar that we don't even know we could live without them. And here's the thing: the ego doesn't want us to find that out.

There's a reason the prayer is not "Please *help me* heal these fear-based thoughts." Why? Because most of us are lousy at evicting fear. We need to have it done for us. In fact, our job is to get out of the way. But this is not relinquishment of duty; this is admitting that our thoughts are the problem. If we try to fix our fear-based thoughts with more fear-based thoughts, they'll just circle around, smack us in the face all over again and throw an empty potato chip bag on the floor.

## Why the words "fear-based?"

Because those words cast a wide net, making us aware of the countless thoughts that are rooted in fear.

If the prayer was, "Please heal my fearful thoughts," we might limit ourselves to threats we *know* we're afraid of, like health scares and things that go bump in the night.

But, as we've already seen, even though fear-based thoughts are rooted in fear, we don't necessarily think of them as arising from fear. Anger, for instance, is always the result of something in me that doesn't feel whole. And, as *A Course*

"The term
'fear-based thoughts'
acknowledges that,
no matter how big
the fear, it is just
a thought, and a
thought can be
changed."

*in Miracles* says, it is nothing more than an attempt to make someone else feel guilty so I can feel better. Maybe yelling will make me feel momentarily more powerful, vindicated, or righteous. But when that wears off—and it will—I'll be right back to the original fear: I'm not enough. By using the term "fear-based," you'll find that more thoughts fall into this bucket than you ever imagined.

Also, the term "fear-based thoughts" acknowledges that, no matter how big the fear, it is just a thought, and a thought can be changed. Fear doesn't originate in the world outside you; it takes shape within your mind—*and then shapes the world as you know it.*

Without the help of the Holy Spirit, you're like a lamp trying to turn itself on. If that lamp isn't plugged into the power it needs, no amount of trying will help. It will fidget and wriggle and swear at the electrical cord, getting increasingly frustrated until it's convinced that light is no longer a possibility. But plug it into the wall where it can draw on its power source, and the frustration immediately disappears. Now it can be in an illumined state.

There is no inherent value in experiencing fear in any form. Leaving it behind is leaving nothing behind. Do not get trapped in the idea that you "should" be experiencing anger and frustration in your life to be fully alive. That is a trick of the ego. And so is the idea that we can fully release fear without the Holy Spirit's help.

# seven

# Paying Attention
# to Your Thoughts

In the days following the CR-V day, I committed to making the prayer my spiritual practice. I would ask for healing, I decided, every time I detected a fear-based thought.

I ended up saying it all day long.

I had thought I was pretty tuned into my thoughts. But once I started becoming aware of fear-based thoughts as soon as they came up, I realized just how pervasive they were. They took endless forms, and they never stopped. For example—

- *I just sneezed. Am I catching a cold? I don't have time to catch a cold.*

- *Bob's late. Is he okay? Is the rain starting to freeze on the roads?*

- *My car oil light came on. How long has it been since I changed the oil? What if it's low and I've damaged the engine?*

- *We need to take the barn cats to be spayed before it's too late.*

- *Why do I always have to be the one who unloads the dishwasher?*

"By asking for
your fear-based
thoughts to be
healed, a new
space is created
within
your mind."

These are seemingly benign thoughts. No rage or huge problems. Just everyday, run-of-the-mill frustration, dissatisfaction, blame, etc. And that's what we all live with all the time, often without even being aware.

Other thoughts speak to our deeper fears, such as—

- *Will I ever find a partner in life? How can I find someone to love me when I'm not lovable?*

- *Life is a constant struggle, and I don't see any way out.*

- *We're on the brink financially. What if we lose everything?*

- *I can't seem to make anyone happy, and the world is going downhill. What's the point of life anyway?*

When we become aware of our thoughts, we can ask that they be healed. That's why paying attention to them is important. Only when you know what you're thinking can you see what a negative impact fear-based thoughts have on your life. Then you can ask for healing instead.

When I found that my mind was WAY more toxic than I'd realized, I approached it the way you would a garden that's filled with weeds: pulling them out one by one and also using a blanket approach.

As they came up, I said the prayer. "Please heal this fear-based thought." And then, every once in a while, I'd throw in a

*Please* heal

**ALL**

*my fear-based*

THOUGHTS.

I was definitely in touch with the Holy Spirit . . . constantly. It was like being on the phone all day. And every time I thought I could hang up for a while . . . oops, another fear-based thought showed up.

As you can see, this requires paying close attention to your thoughts, something that may come easy—or not. I've found that, when we truly tune into our thoughts, we may discover one long stream-of-consciousness honor roll of fear, irritation, negativity and stagnancy, repeating the same ideas over and over.

Using this prayer is not about positive thinking or going into denial or pretending that "bad things" don't matter. Using this prayer is about genuinely and humbly asking for your mind to be healed. This is about freeing yourself from the ego mind that desperately wants to keep you stuck and afraid.

So how *do* you pay attention to your thoughts when you're not used to it? Start by taking a minute to tune in. Begin listening to the chatter in your mind. Listen for the thoughts that make your mind seem like a pinball machine— the ones that glance off the sides and roll around, bouncing over and over again.

"Using this prayer is about genuinely and humbly asking for your mind to be healed."

Several techniques can help you focus on what's inside your head.

Try journaling—simply sit with a paper and pen (or in front of the computer) and record everything that rolls through your mind for five or ten minutes.

Go for a walk by yourself and tune into your thoughts.

Or turn off the radio while you're driving and pay attention to what you think about.

Check in at key times of the day, too:

What are your first thoughts in the morning and the last ones at night?

What are you thinking as you leave the house or arrive home?

What floats through your mind when you're alone?

When you're with another person?

There's no need to judge these thoughts or try to change them. Just be aware of them as though you were watching a parade go by. *"Huh, look at that—another fear-based thought about money."*

And if you're not sure whether a thought is fear-based or not, do this easy test. Ask yourself: *Does this thought make me feel light and free, or does it make me feel heavy and tired?* With this test, most fear-based thoughts will reveal themselves for what they are.

You can also pay attention to your body. Maybe you're not aware of the thought, but you are aware of the gnawing fear you feel in your stomach. That's a pretty sure sign.

Truthfully, most of us don't go through our days worrying about nuclear disaster. Instead, our heads are filled with thoughts about paying the gas bill and whether we're going to disappoint someone we care about.

The constant irritation from those more mundane fears is like the sharp-edged tag in the back of a sweater, scratching the base of your neck all day. You don't even realize how annoyed you are until you get home, rip off the sweater, and throw it in the laundry, wondering why you've been in a bad mood for the past twelve hours.

But when we're in this state of unconscious upset and a *bigger* issue comes along, we don't have the emotional reserves to deal with it. Or we overreact to any little aggravation.

As you get better at tuning into your thoughts, you'll become more aware of the ways fear impacts your psyche, and how you make decisions based on fear without even knowing you're doing it.

For example, a young couple recently bought a new house. Thrilled about being first-time homeowners, they brought in the last load of belongings to the house, then went out with their one-year-old to celebrate. When they returned later that evening, they found that their house had been burglarized. They'd lost several irreplaceable items, including two one-of-a-kind folk banjos. Even some of their baby's clothes were gone.

They started asking themselves and God why this had happened. Had they done something wrong? Did they bring this upon themselves? Were they being punished because they were so excited about the house? In other words, at the same time they wanted to lash out at the thieves, they lashed out at themselves from guilt and blame.

This is a common fear-based response, handing the ego evidence that the world is a scary, dangerous place—a place where you can't trust anybody. But the more insidious

"Ask yourself:

*Does this thought*

*make me feel light and*

*free, or does it make*

*me feel heavy*

*and tired?"*

message is this: "See? You were excited and happy about that new home, and look what happened!" With that, a piece of you decides that joy invites punishment. That's the fearful ego talking.

When you listen to that fearful ego, you become suspicious of everyone and never allow yourself to be fully happy. At that point, the ultimate irony occurs: You think you've made yourself safe from harm, but you've actually imprisoned yourself.

By asking for your fear-based thoughts to be healed, you start with a clean slate. A new space is created within your mind. And in that moment, you change your entire future, because you're no longer defined by the lingering fear of the past.

# eight

# What Can You Expect When You Start?

**Y**our experience with the prayer will be as unique as you are. When you start saying it, you may see some instant changes in your own fears or external circumstances, or you may see none at all. There is no schedule, no blueprint, no one way to do this. Just start noticing your thoughts and saying the prayer, and see what happens.

With that said, here are a few things that *might* happen for you. Again, let go of any expectations and become a witness. And commit to saying the prayer regularly for at least two weeks before you evaluate your experience with it.

## You may be excited about this at first and then experience a quick crash of enthusiasm.

This happens because the prayer speaks to your higher Self, which sees the value of it and knows that it will make a difference over time. But then the loud two-year-old ego, whose voice easily drowns out the quiet higher Self, gets in your face and says, "Not so fast!" Your ego will resist in every possible way. It will try to make you forget the prayer, and it will ridicule it and tell you it's not working. It will try to make you fall asleep or get sick with a bad case of the flu. It will manufacture crises or major turmoil. It will create an overwhelming sense of angst or failure just when you thought things were looking up in your life. It will use every tool in its toolbox to make you think this is a stupid, worthless waste of time *because of all the things it's scared of.* Your ego is afraid that your relationships will change—that you'll find the love of your life, you'll end an unhealthy relationship, or you'll experience more peace with the people around you. Your ego is afraid you'll pay off your bills and build your savings account. It's afraid you'll fulfill your life purpose. It's afraid that you won't listen to it, that it won't be in charge. Most of all, it's afraid that you'll grow and be truly happy.

So, what should you do if you find yourself resisting the prayer? Do it anyway. Write out the prayer and tape it to your dashboard. Write it on your bathroom mirror. Place it next to your bed so you'll see it first thing in the morning and last thing at night. Or, as one woman did, write it on dozens of slips of paper and post them all over the house.

No matter what boulders your ego throws in your path, it's essential to continue saying the prayer, to keep asking for your fear-based thoughts to be healed. Remember: Using the prayer is a practice, not a magic bullet.

## *You may find new reasons to use the prayer every day.*

As you go through your day, whenever you're about to embark on a new activity, take a moment to stop and say, "Please heal my fear-based thoughts." You might be headed toward a meeting, planning an important conversation with a family member, or simply getting in the car to run errands. Whatever it is, take a breath and ask for your fear-based thoughts to be healed. When you do this regularly, you'll find that feelings of stress, worry, or anxiety will diminish, and you'll experience your days with greater peace of mind.

## *You may be surprised at the fear messages coming from outside you.*

You'll start to tune in and hear the world's chatter differently, including the evening news, headlines on the Internet, and the gossip coming from the next cubicle. You may be surprised at

"Mind chatter is largely made up of fear. Keep using the prayer, and the tidal wave of fear-based thoughts will gradually subside."

the diet of drama you've been ingesting without even knowing it, and you may decide to limit your exposure to fear-based thinking and teaching.

## *You may be surprised at the fear messages coming from inside you.*

You'll see that mind chatter is largely made up of fear. You may become aware of how addicted you've been to it, and how toxic the thoughts are. At first, when the fear-based thoughts seem relentless, you may feel like you're trying to sweep the ocean away with a broom. Keep using the prayer, and the tidal wave of fear-based thoughts will gradually subside.

## *You may see light where you thought there was darkness.*

Over the years of working with people in personal growth classes, I've heard many ask some form of this question: "What if I look inside my heart and it's filled with snakes and darkness?" And my response is this: "Invariably, if you look inside your heart, you will find doves and light." We fear the process of self-discovery because our egos have us convinced that we *are* our fear-based thoughts. But when those thoughts are healed, our essence as children of God is revealed. When you start to use the prayer, you'll put the key in the lock of a door that scares you. But keep your eyes open; you'll be amazed at the beauty on the other side of that door.

## *Your ego may set up a hierarchy of fear-based thoughts.*

It may start to tell you, for instance, that fear about an ill child is important, but fear about forgetting someone's name at a party is not. In the external world, there is a difference. But internally, they both interfere with your peace of mind.

Similarly, the ego will turn misery into a competition, as in: "No one has suffered as much as I have. No one can possibly know the pain I've endured." The truth, of course, is that everyone experiences loss, illness, financial setbacks, issues with loved ones, natural disasters, and a host of other challenges. Holding onto struggle as a badge of honor is another ego device to make you feel separate, significant, and stuck.

If you start dismissing fears because they're not big enough—or because they're bigger than anyone else's—remind yourself that those are judgments of the ego. The peace of God is your goal, so anything that stands between you and that peace is ripe for healing.

## *You may feel disoriented.*

Remember, the ego is like a scared little kid. Using this prayer is like starting the daily lessons in the "Workbook for Students" that's part of *A Course in Miracles*. The lessons are designed to loosen your attachments to everything you think has meaning in your life and empty out your old belief system so that love can take the place of fear.

Years ago, I interviewed students at a seminary for a writing project. They described a similar process, one in which their old beliefs were wiped clean so they could build a belief system that was authentic to them. I noticed an interesting pattern among them. The first-year students were optimistic. The third-year students were wise. But the second-year students looked like their dog had just been shot. In that limbo state between old beliefs and new, they felt lost and adrift.

"The only way to

heal old wounds

is to acknowledge

them, not to lock

them up."

You may not experience anything quite so dramatic. But because the prayer is a complete threat to the ego, don't be surprised if that part of you starts throwing louder tantrums. This will affect you on many levels: spiritual, mental, emotional, and physical. You may feel tired, dehydrated, and dizzy. But, as uncomfortable as it may be, this is a good sign. Take good care of yourself, and keep saying the prayer.

## *Your heart may open.*

This process may release emotions and past hurts that you don't want to feel, which is why the ego keeps your heart closed. It thinks it's protecting you this way. But the only way to heal old wounds is to acknowledge them, not to lock them up. In fact, as long as your ego keeps your emotions imprisoned, you'll be held hostage. Let yourself admit the hurts so they can be healed, and you'll find peace of mind on the other side.

## *Your ego may create new forms*
## *of the same problem.*

For example: Marilyn has been married more than twenty years and is frustrated with her husband. She feels he's critical about her weight, her intelligence, the way she cooks—pretty much everything about her. When we talked about the root cause of the problem, and how important it is for her to value herself more, I could see a particular look in her eyes. It was the look of the ego saying, "*Uh-oh. Who* else *can I blame this problem on?*" Immediately she started talking about a sister who doesn't listen to her and makes her feel invisible. Same problem, different form.

As you start to use the prayer, your ego will be more insistent than ever about looking outside yourself for the source of the problem, someone to blame—just as I did on CR-V day when I wanted to pin the rattles on the body shop manager or Bob.

"The majority of fear-based thoughts can be traced back to guilt, shame, and self-judgment . . .

. . . all of which close us off from the most unique and vibrant parts of ourselves."

## *You may feel that a new space opens up inside you.*

Many people tell me that when they first say the prayer, their internal landscape immediately changes. One woman— someone who listens to God *a lot*—told me that, as she said the prayer for the first time, she heard Spirit saying to her, "FINALLY. Now we can really get some things done!"

Another woman, who lives in Mexico, was so inspired and freed by the prayer that she sat down and started writing a memoir that had been gestating for years. "I have always been afraid of rejection, humiliation, and ridicule," she says. "I lived with them all my life. So here is my challenge to step out and take the chance. I actually feel at peace with it."

And a woman in Montana said this of the prayer: "It has calmed me when I've felt agitation and has given me rest when I've been awakened from sleep. I have it posted in my workspace and in my home and delight in sharing it with others who express need for such relief."

## *You may experience a new level of self-acceptance.*

The majority of fear-based thoughts can be traced back to guilt, shame, and self-judgment, all of which close us off from the most unique and vibrant parts of ourselves. It takes courage to be all of who you are in a world that runs on conformity, which is why the prayer can be the tool to set you free. You may feel drawn to a career path that no one expects. Or a talent that you've kept hidden. Or a way of expressing yourself through clothes or music that you've never revealed. Or a secret about abuse that you've never shared. Or a sexual orientation that you're afraid will cut you off from family or friends. Ask yourself: *What part of myself have I kept in the closet?* Then ask for your fear-based thoughts about it to be healed. At first, you may experience brief moments of recovery, as though your oxygen has been restored. Keep using the prayer until those moments turn into long, deep breaths of self-awareness and love.

*nine*

# What Happens
# Over Time?

Asking for your fear-based thoughts to be healed has a cumulative effect. Not only will you experience more peace of mind, but your tolerance for fear-based thoughts may diminish as well. When those thoughts do come up, it will become easier to recognize them, ask for them to be healed, and change your focus to loving thoughts, so you can experience more joy, abundance, and well-being.

What else can you expect after you've used the prayer for a while?

## *Peace of mind will become your only goal.*

This flies in the face of everything fear teaches us or wants us to believe. Our egos want us to think that to be happy we need that house, that car, that iPad, that *whatever*, and so we strive and work and train and finagle and cajole our way to buy the things we think we need. And where love is concerned, things can be equally distorted. Having grown up hearing stories of romantic tragedy, we may think love is real only if it's tenuous or complicated.

In fact, we are bombarded by messages that tell us our goal is to be promoted . . . or to be seen as successful . . . or to compete well . . . or to win . . . or to have more stuff in our garage than the folks down the street do. We are *not* bombarded by messages that say, "What if you just went for peace of mind?"

When that thought first enters your consciousness as a real possibility, your ego is likely to say, "How boring is *that?*" But when you start to seriously entertain the prospect of a peaceful mind, you find that in it lies your strength and true happiness. You move to an internal state of well-being that is no longer determined by what you have or whom you know, and you start to feel impervious to fear—not because you've built barriers to danger, but because you've dismantled the barriers to love.

Ironically, in this place, everything you've been seeking in the external world may show up. The love of your life, the perfect job, physical well-being, financial stability, clarity about your life direction—all of them now are free to flow into your life because, in asking for your fear-based thoughts to be healed, you no longer need the lesson, and the rattles disappear.

## *You'll see more beauty in the world.*

Imagine that you're in a Japanese garden filled with bonsai trees, exotic foliage, and graceful footbridges crossing gentle streams. Now imagine that someone has walked their dog in the garden and left a pile of crap on the grass. Your ego wants you to focus on that pile. It will make you angry about it. "Who would defile this place?" your ego will ask. "Somebody could step in it. There should be laws about these things!"

Meanwhile, at the same time that you're getting more upset and channeling anger from the Fear Tree, dozens of people are wandering through the Japanese garden, focusing their attention on how exquisite it is.

This is our choice in life. The ego wants us to stay glued to the pile of crap, oblivious to the beauty in the world around us. In fact, when your attention is diverted by a flowering tree or a shaft of light on a blooming shrub, your ego will pull you right back with another reason to be upset about the pile in front of you.

But when you ask for your fear-based thoughts to be healed, the ego's spell is broken, and you become free to wander through the garden. A caretaker might come and clean up the pile—or you might even dispose of it yourself. In either case, the pile will have no power over you. Why would it? You'll be busy enjoying the beauty that's been there all along.

## You'll open up to the divine.

One man who was experiencing financial issues started using the prayer and found that he was better able to "listen for what my best actions need to be." Using the prayer consistently quiets the mind so you not only can listen, but you can hear and discern actions that come from love rather than from fear—in other words, actions that will help you expand and extend love in the world.

## You'll experience greater simplicity and serendipity.

Life situations will work out without effort on your part, reminding you that, because fear is not standing in your way, you are free to experience the universe's natural flow of abundance and ease. You may have had these kinds

"Using the prayer consistently quiets the mind so you can hear and discern actions that come from love rather than from fear."

of experiences in the past. You'll think you're late for an appointment—until you find that the person you're meeting got hung up in traffic and arrived at exactly the same time you did. Or you'll need money to take a class that's outside your budget, and it will show up in the most unexpected way. One woman found two $100 bills in a book she'd bought from a half-price bookstore. She'd had the book on her shelf for a year and was part of the way through reading it before the money fell out in front of her. She spent the unexpected cash on a writing class she'd wanted to take, which has since led to a profound change in her life direction. These instances of serendipity will multiply as you say the prayer, affirming that everything is possible with love.

## *You may experience other pathways to healing.*

Because the prayer shifts you to a place of greater peace and harmony, practicing it makes other healing possible. It's a lot like when you have a migraine and can't think clearly. When the migraine goes away, you experience great clarity. Decisions are easier. You can see things for what they are.

Calming the pain, quieting it down, and feeling it go away allows you to relax into your life and make decisions from a very different place than when the pain is inflamed, filling your mind with hurt.

## *You'll set yourself free by relinquishing control.*

We spend an enormous amount of energy trying to control our relationships, our jobs, our health, our finances, our To Do lists—essentially, the world around us. Not only is this exhausting, it keeps us trapped in chronic fear that if we let up, things will fall apart. And what happens if everything does crumble around us? We feel guilty. We think we've failed. The spin cycle of fear goes into hyperdrive.

This is why pivotal moments of "letting go" often come at a time of crisis. We may face a life-threatening illness, divorce, bankruptcy, or other life-changing circumstance. Or maybe we just get to the point where we realize we're not large and in charge, and we're weary from pretending we are. At these moments, we may finally turn to God and ask for help.

There's a wonderful passage in *A Course in Miracles* about the reason we fight so hard for the illusion of control—and what we discover when we finally surrender. It says, ". . . you believe that without the ego, all would be chaos. Yet I assure you that without the ego, all would be love."

Ask for your fear-based thoughts to be healed, and you allow divine energy to direct your life. It's much more peaceful, and it's also a constant delight to see how perfectly things can be orchestrated when we get out of the way.

## *You may understand yourself and your relationship to God on a deeper level.*

My nephew, a highly spiritual young man, was doing research on plant genetics in his first job out of college. He started using the prayer and typically felt immediate relief. Then, one day, he had an experience at work that took the prayer to a different level.

It seems he had an idea about improving a project, and he asked a co-worker for her opinion about it. He was eager to mention the idea to his boss to improve his standing in the department.

My nephew left the room for a couple minutes and came back to find his associate presenting the idea to their boss and taking full credit for it. Feeling he'd been left in the dust, my nephew felt the anger start to rise within him. "It was palpable," he said. "I'd been robbed of some acclaim, and my ego was winning."

When he had a few minutes to himself, he sat down, closed his eyes, and asked for his fear-based thoughts to be healed. Instead of getting immediate relief this time, he felt like he entered into a dialogue with the Holy Spirit. He was prompted to look at where the anger came from and how it was rooted in fear.

When he did that, he traced the anger back to its beginnings. "I had thought that impressing my boss was important," he said, *as if I weren't already perfect and complete as I am.*"

Bingo. By spending time with the prayer and that inner dialogue, he remembered who he is as a child of God. Not only did he experience peace, he now understood himself and his relationship to God in a new way.

This is an excellent example of the message I received on CR-V day—that when our fear-based thinking is healed, the triggers for the fear are no longer needed. In this case, the prayer helped my nephew come face to face with his own value. By recognizing himself as whole and complete, he moves forward with greater confidence as a child of God, making it less likely he'll experience similar situations in the future.

## *You'll be better able to fulfill your purpose.*

I've seen people struggle with the question of "What's my purpose?" almost more than any other. Without a mission propelling you forward, it's easy to get weary and apathetic about life. But how do you find that purpose—and fulfill it— if it's hidden under layers of fear? Those layers may include feelings of *What will others think? Will this be acceptable? Who am I to want this? Do I deserve it? It's too late for me. I've been bored/overworked/taking care of others for so long that I don't know what I want anymore.*

Because finding and fulfilling your purpose means being true to yourself and choosing the path that's right for you, it's an enormous threat to your ego. No wonder so many people struggle with this aspect of their lives. When you experience yourself and your life through the lens of fear, you'll see roadblocks everywhere. But when you ask for those fear-based thoughts to be healed, you'll see answers start to emerge, and the universe will deliver support from the most unexpected places.

## *You'll take a more direct path to joy.*

One woman recently wrote to me saying she's done years of spiritual practice and self-growth. She's been to therapists, healers, and classes, and she's read countless self-help books. Each of them gave her tools, she said, "but none of them taught me how to be happy."

That's because they're missing the simplest and most effective tool of all—asking the Holy Spirit to heal the root cause of their unhappiness: fear-based thinking. I can say that with confidence because I missed it for years. Even with spiritual practice—something that by its very nature should rely on divine intervention—it's easy to overlook that one key ingredient. In fact, when the prayer first showed up in my life, I had a "duh" moment—I recognized that the help I

126

needed had been right there all along. I just hadn't seen it or remembered that asking for it could be so easy.

Let's say, for instance, that you read a book about the law of attraction. You're excited about manifesting your dreams—and then your ego takes over. *Well, sure, that may work for everyone else, but not for me.* That's the ego's way of saying, "I'm different and alone, I'm not good enough, and I'm not worthy." Until those thoughts are healed, it's going to be very difficult to create the life you want, because your fears will be there, blocking the door.

So, if you're using affirmations, positive self-talk, meditation, journaling, or other tools for self-knowledge, keep going. But if, at the same time, you also ask for your fear-based thoughts to be healed, you'll take a significant shortcut on your inner journey.

## You'll be better able to live in the now.

Most of our fears are tied to the past or future. That's why living in the present moment is so desirable—and seems so difficult to do for a sustained period. If you try to fully experience the now, you'll probably find you can maintain your focus for a short time, until your attention gets diverted—most likely by fear. You'll start worrying about whether you fed the cats before you left the house, or where you stashed the dry-cleaning ticket, or if you've forgotten someone's birthday. As you use the prayer consistently, though, you may find that you spend more time in the present because your mind isn't cluttered with so many fear-based distractions.

## You'll trade perfectionism for perfection.

Perfectionism comes from the ego. Perfection comes from God. Perfectionism is the fear that you're not good enough and have to prove your worth by not making a mistake. Perfection is the truth that you're complete and whole as you are.

By using the prayer consistently, you become aware that, as the *Course* says, "Nothing you do or think or wish or make is necessary to establish your worth."

## You'll feel grateful.

As you feel the peace of God within, you'll be filled with thankfulness. And because you'll be saying "please" a lot,

"Perfectionism comes from the ego. Perfection comes from God."

you will naturally want to say "thank you." It's impossible to be grateful and have fear-based thoughts simultaneously. The very act of saying "thank you" will support the healing of the prayer in a significant way. Just imagine what this does to transform the focus of your thoughts and, therefore, your entire being. You start saying the prayer over and over, and each time you say it, you follow it with an automatic expression of thanks. This is like throwing crystals in a toxic stream. Before long, the water can't help but become more pure, reflecting the light with greater clarity.

## You'll be satisfied.

A lot of fear comes from that indefinable word "enough." Am I thin enough? Do we have enough money? Is our car new enough? Are we successful enough? To the fear-based ego, nothing is ever enough, which breeds endless dissatisfaction. Ask for your fear-based thoughts to be healed, and you'll remember that you are enough. That's where you'll find peace of mind.

"You are enough."

## You'll focus less on where the fear came from and more on healing it.

Trying to figure out why we feel dissatisfied, can't find love, don't feel enthused about life, worry excessively, or experience any other issues may be instructive, but it may also be the ego's way of keeping us so focused on the fear that we never get past it. Searching for the cause can become part of the struggle, another setting in the spin cycle of fear. Remember that you don't need to know what prompted the fear-based thoughts; all you need is a willingness for them to be healed.

## You'll experience more love in your life.

When you ask for fear-based thoughts to be healed, you remove the barriers that stand in the way of love.

This happened for me years ago when I'd been divorced for fifteen years and was tired of flunking Relationships 101 over and over again. I kept attracting the same man in a slightly different package—sometimes bald, sometimes funny, sometimes successful—but always, ultimately, unavailable.

"When you use the prayer consistently, you can give and receive love without fear getting in the way."

Finally one day, in conversation with God, I acknowledged that I was clueless and didn't know how to find the right man for me. What I thought I *wanted* in a partner and what I actually *needed* in a partner were clearly different, and I didn't have the benefit of the bigger picture to see who that person might be. Even though I didn't have the words for it then, I was asking for my fear-based thoughts about myself and my right relationship to be healed.

I clearly remember the moment I finally relinquished that control to a higher power. I experienced the sense of relief and immediate comfort you feel when someone steps in and says, "Thanks for asking. Let me take it from here." Sure enough, five weeks later, after years of fear-based dating, I met Bob. And as CR-V day demonstrated, we're not only excellent partners, we're both teachers and students for one another on a spiritual level.

It seems very simple now. Before I asked for help, I operated from fear. So what did I find? Relationships based on fear. After asking for help, the barriers to love disintegrated. So what did I find? Love.

When you use the prayer consistently, you can give and receive love without fear getting in the way.

## *You may become more honest and vulnerable.*

*A Course in Miracles* says that your vulnerability is your strength. That's because, in your vulnerability, you can be who you truly are without judging yourself or fearing the judgment of others.

Our fear of judgment takes different forms. We may become pleasers—setting impossibly high expectations for ourselves, saying what we think others want to hear, and deep-sixing our own desires in order to make everyone else happy. Or we may go the other direction, arrogantly promoting ourselves as better than others and painting an exaggerated picture of who we are. *A Course in Miracles* calls these two expressions "littleness" and "grandiosity." Despite the fact that they look different, both are branches of the same Fear Tree.

When you ask for your fear-based thoughts to be healed, you pave the way for "grandeur," an expression of who you

"The more you
acknowledge
positive changes,
the more positive
changes will occur."

are as a child of God. With no need to prove your worth, justify your existence, or hide your gifts, you stand in grace and peace, knowing it's safe to simply be yourself.

## You'll see glimpses of change in your world.

Some changes may be subtle, some may be much larger and more pronounced. You may see them in yourself, the people around you, or in your life circumstances. Pay attention when the rattles in your dashboard disappear, even though your ego will downplay such moments. Look for the miracle. It may not happen instantaneously, but that doesn't mean things aren't shifting.

In fact, the more you acknowledge positive changes—no matter how slight—without doubting them, the more positive changes will occur. Consider keeping a journal of changes to help track shifts you might otherwise overlook. This will also help you counteract the ego's urging to abandon the prayer.

## *You'll become more forgiving.*

You may believe there are some things that can't be forgiven. But lack of forgiveness perpetuates separation. It keeps you mired in anger, where peace of mind cannot exist. And it cuts you off from receiving the forgiveness of others. Because of this, your lack of forgiveness doesn't punish the other person—it simply imprisons you.

Refusing to forgive means digging in your heels and trading joy for a sense of righteousness. This is so prevalent in our world that when we see an example of forgiveness we're stunned by it. Consider the Amish community in Pennsylvania that forgave the man who shot ten of their schoolgirls, then built the New Hope School as a sign of reconciliation. Or Ronald Cotton, a man who, wrongly imprisoned for rape and later freed after a DNA test, harbored no anger toward his accuser and, in fact, co-wrote a book with her about judicial reform. We often consider such instances of forgiveness anomalies, as though they are the acts of superheroes.

But what if forgiveness were the norm rather than the exception? Immediately your ego will say, "Then everybody would feel free to do anything they wanted." But people attack because they're afraid. A more forgiving world would be a world of less fear and, ultimately, a world of less attack.

Making a choice to forgive means asking yourself, "Would I rather be right or would I rather be happy?" Before you pay for someone else's fear-based actions by being angry for the rest of your life, ask for your fear-based thoughts to be healed. You may be surprised by a space in both your mind and heart for a different belief—as well as the return of joy.

## *You may have a greater sense of being on solid ground.*

At one time in my life I felt like a Whac-A-Mole. Every time my head popped above ground, I got whacked on the head. No wonder I thought the world was a scary place.

By the time I started saying this prayer, I'd done enough spiritual work that I instead felt like an inflatable toy that's tied to a foundation. I might get knocked over from time to time, but I'd always pop right back up again.

But just a couple of weeks after starting the prayer, I felt like that inflatable toy had been set free and was now floating on the surface of water. I was bouncing around a little but staying upright, being carried by the currents.

A big reason for this shift is that the prayer healed my self-judgment. Typically we spend more time than we realize playing a role in order to make others happy. We think we do this because we don't want others to judge us, but we're actually doing it because we're judging ourselves. *Who am I to follow my own path, speak my mind, or say no?* When that fear is healed, we fulfill one of my favorite statements: *What other people think of me is none of my business.* In other words, we stop taking things personally. We live in our own spiritual strength. We become like Teflon, so the fears of others slide right off us. In that place, we are unshakable, truly on solid ground.

Now, instead of my thoughts focusing on what other people think, I can focus on the question, "Am I at peace?" And if the answer is no, the issue is not, "What can I fix or how can I make them happy?" It's . . .

*Please*

# heal

*my*

*fear-based*

THOUGHTS.

# ten

# How Does the Prayer Work in Real Life?

**F**ear is powerful stuff. It can be so subtle and wear so many different disguises, we may not know what we're dealing with. It can put the brakes on our lives, cause us to stay too long in situations that don't serve us, and prevent us from making decisions that can move us forward.

To help you recognize areas of your life in which fear may be more present than you think, here are several situations in which fear has played a major role. Even if your circumstances are different from these, use the suggestion at the end of each story to think of an area in your life in which the prayer can support you.

FOR MOST PEOPLE, the idea of losing their job, going through foreclosure, having a chronic health condition, or experiencing a change in family relationships would be enough to send them into a tailspin of fear. But imagine facing *all four* of those challenges at the same time—and yet feeling calmer than ever through it all. That was the case for Shelley, who attended a workshop about *The Only Little Prayer You Need* on the eve of being laid off from her corporate job.

For several months, Shelley's boss had tried to intimidate her into quitting her job, which would have saved the company a severance package. Every day she woke up dreading going to the office knowing how she'd be subjected yet again to her boss's fear-based tactics.

At the same time, Shelley and her husband were trying to sell their house, but they learned there were severe structural problems with the older bungalow, which they now lovingly call the Titanic. Because it would cost far more to repair the house than it's worth, they'd decided to do a short sale and possibly a foreclosure, which would be a source of embarrassment, not to mention uncertainty about where they and their elementary-school-aged daughter will live.

As if that weren't enough, Shelley has Graves disease, an autoimmune disorder that affects the thyroid and saps her energy. And she recently learned that her mother will be moving in with them at the Titanic due to unexpected changes in her own living situation.

It may look as though the rattles in Shelley's dashboard haven't disappeared since she came to the workshop and started using the prayer. In fact, it may seem that they've multiplied. Yet her husband noticed that she smiles more now than ever. Why? "I'm calmer than I've ever been," she says.

"I use the prayer on an hourly basis, even minute to minute," Shelley says. "It's almost a sense of empowerment and great courage. In the past, I felt like I was scared all the time, making rash decisions based on fear. But when you slow down and the fear is healed and you experience peace, you make better decisions."

Because she's no longer running on fear, Shelley trusts that the right job will come along, and she's exploring ideas for starting her own business. "Five years ago I would have jumped at the first job offer and been totally miserable after six months," she says. "Now I'm able to take a step back, look at the fear, and ask for healing."

Shelley's inner peace has impacted her family too. "I feel like I'm a calmer person, so I'm projecting more calm to my family," she says. "Whatever you're projecting can affect your whole household."

Her husband understands the prayer in a different way. When Shelley came home from the prayer workshop, she told him all about it and shared the list of fears she'd written

"The prayer changes our minds so we can live with peace, no matter what's going on around us."

as part of that experience. Then she handed him a blank sheet of paper and asked him to do the same thing. They weren't surprised to find that many of the same fears showed up on both of their lists.

Neither of them expected to deal with so many challenges at once, but Shelley believes in the adage that God doesn't give you more than you can handle. Now she knows the power of having her fear healed.

"I know that God is working in my life. It may not be according to my schedule or going exactly the way I want, but I know He's there and He's working. The prayer has given me faith to know everything is going to be okay. There's no need to be fearful about anything. I don't think I'll ever go back to being scared Shelley again."

Shelley's story illustrates the power of this prayer to make a true miracle happen: the prayer changes our minds so we can live with peace, no matter what's going on around us.

I doubt that anyone would blame Shelley if she got angry, depressed, or overwhelmed right now. In fact, the world has programmed her to do so. Isn't a job the source of your security? Isn't a house the source of shelter and comfort? How could you lose both and be calm about it?

This is why the prayer works in real life: it replaces the artificial sources of security, shelter, and comfort in our lives with the real thing—remembrance of our connection to God, which is our true abundance.

Shelley is still dealing with challenges, but the *way* she's dealing with them has changed. The externals in her life no longer have power over her. Now it's all about living from a more peaceful center, supported by Spirit.

If you're facing the loss of a job, home, or relationship that gives you a sense of security, ask for this: *Please heal my fear-based thoughts about the future so I can experience comfort and security from my true Source.*

A FRIEND IN TEXAS is writing a book that she wants to sell on the Internet, launching a business that will carry her into retirement. A journalist, she has won more awards for her investigative stories than she can fit on one wall, so she's not afraid to tackle difficult subjects or walk into new situations. But when she received an email from a well-known Internet marketer about a training that would be ideal for her, her ego went to work:

- *You'll have to fly to New York and book a hotel. That's a lot of money.*

- *If you wait, the training will probably be offered on video for a lot less.*

- *Develop the product first and test it—then go to a training for guidance when you have something tangible to look at.*

- *You'll probably be the only woman there, or the only person under seventy. What if you're bored? What if this is just not your group?*

Her ego generated an entire laundry list of fears and objections, and all of them looked like perfectly logical reasons to stay home. But something in her wanted to say yes. Something about this event affirmed her desire to express herself in a way that's true to the core of her being, creating something of value that will carry her through the rest of her life with joy.

This is the trap of the ego. While the ego sometimes sounds like a two-year-old who hasn't slept for days, it can also sound like an accountant wearing sensible shoes. It can tick off all the reasons to stay small, and they will make sense to you because they're exactly what many of your friends and relatives would say. *Oh, that's WAY too much money! It's such a risk . . . what if it's not worth it? It's going to be freezing in Manhattan at that time of year, and you don't even own a winter coat.* All of these excuses sound perfectly sensible, but what the ego is really saying is this: "I'm terrified that you will learn, grow, and find more joy. I will do everything I can to keep you locked in the status quo, and I will be very crafty about it by making it seem like it's in your own best interests."

That's how we stay small, bored, and unhappy.

The thing is, true joy doesn't come from following a backup plan. It comes from doing the thing you're afraid to do. In fact, if you're afraid to do it, it's a pretty good sign that that's exactly what you *should* do, because it would nourish your higher Self.

You can try to talk yourself out of the fear. Or you can ask the Holy Spirit to heal your fear-based thoughts and start living with joy today.

> If you're afraid to take a risk and move forward, ask for this: *Please heal my fear-based thoughts about doing what I love so I can create the life of my dreams.*

MAYBE ONE OF THE MOST-ASKED questions about this prayer is this: "How can the prayer help me when I've gone through a loss? What if someone I love has died, an important relationship has ended, or I've gone through a life-changing crisis? Isn't it normal to feel grief and anger?"

Absolutely. Here's how one young person expressed the question.

"Well, what happens if the worst fears have already come to pass? For me personally that means that my smarts, athleticism, and social abilities all got taken from me in a car wreck that wasn't even my fault. After giving basically the entirety of my adolescence to a youth group [I'm twenty-five now], I head off to college to study and, in one moment, my life basically got ruined because of another driver. And now what? I still spend four days a week in therapy, and there's not really all that much hope that it's going to be changing any day soon."

Here's what I believe: God is not an entity who dispenses judgment or punishment, or who lets bad things happen to good people. Instead, I believe that God is love. And because we're children of God, we are love as well.

In this world, though, we face all sorts of challenges in which anger and grief are natural. But if you can ask for your fears to be healed—fears about what your life will look like, what you will and won't be able to do, how you can ever *not* be angry again—you can open the door to joy.

Again, this is not about just thinking happy thoughts and hoping things will change. It's about asking for a deep and profound healing from a higher power so that you can experience peace in your mind and heart again.

In that place of peace, life is restored. Not because your body—or the person or relationship you lost—changes. But because your remembrance of love is restored. As you remember the child of God you are, peace of mind becomes possible once again.

> If you're dealing with grief and anger, ask for this: *Please heal my fear-based thoughts about my loss so that I can live with joy again.*

LOVE RELATIONSHIPS MAY be more rife with fear than almost any other area of our lives. One of the stories I tell in my prayer workshops goes as follows: I was a voracious reader as a child, and the books that impressed themselves on me the most were stories of unrequited love. I read the ending to *Gone With the Wind* over and over again, trying to *will* Rhett to come back to Scarlett. I consumed *Love Story* in one sitting one night when I stayed at my best friend's house, and the two of us saw the movie twice. We never knew what Jenny died of, but we were sure Oliver loved her because we could see the pain in his eyes.

By the time I was a teenager, the programming was complete: love meant loss, sacrifice, and heartache—all first-class forms of fear. And so, when a man showed up in my life, I would assume that he would leave one day. And—here comes the fun part—I would sabotage the relationship just to give him a little nudge. Then I could say, "See? There are no good men out there!"—when in fact my ego had choreographed the whole thing out of fear.

Then Bob came along. After we'd dated about three months, he'd already taught me that I'd stay warmer if I actually *buttoned* my coat rather than clutching it closed with one hand, and he'd volunteered to weather-strip my house because, after all, winter was coming, I was strapped for cash, and it would save me money if he could reduce my heating bills. I'd been led to a White Knight in a Dodge Caravan—a man who wore a navy blue sweater with his company's emblem stitched on the breast, and who carried little to-do-list slips of paper in his pocket that he actually completed and threw away.

This is why I had to try to sabotage the relationship. It couldn't be love without duress, could it?

My ego went to work on the day when Bob and I were going to see the Lipitor Stallions perform. (They're not really called the Lipitor Stallions, but the name starts with *L* and is hard to remember, so I call the Stallions by their "pharmaceutical" name.) Before Bob and I left for the show, I found something to be upset with him about. And while we sat through the performance, my ego became more indignant and outraged by the minute. By the time the Stallions took their final synchronized bow, I was in tears.

On the way home, I couldn't stop crying. But I realized that the tears weren't out of my trumped-up anger toward

Bob. I was crying because I didn't want this relationship to end. And, given the way I was acting, Bob would have been perfectly justified in opening the passenger door, shoving me out of the van, and driving off with his toolbox and never speaking to me again.

"I'm just afraid one of us will do something to destroy this relationship," I said between sobs, sounding a lot like I had on those rainy days reading *Gone With the Wind*. "And I don't want it to end."

"Well," Bob said, his deep voice soft and reassuring. "I don't see a lack of willingness on either of our parts to make this relationship work."

Whoa. I'd just come face to face with real love. Not the playing-in-the-snow kind from *Love Story* or the "I don't give a damn" kind from *Gone With the Wind*. But the steadfast kind that has your back even when you're acting insane.

I had always thought men had abandoned me. But now I could see that I was the one who had left, devising plots to drive them away, justifying in my mind that they'd done something unforgivable, then passing more months bemoaning the lack of available men in the world.

But in this relationship, Bob wasn't playing the game, so I couldn't either. In the face of forgiveness and understanding, fear was outmatched that day, and a new definition of love took its place.

If you're not experiencing the love relationship you want in your life, ask for this: *Please heal my fear-based thoughts about my own self worth so I can have the true and steadfast love I deserve.*

A LIFE-CHANGING ILLNESS can be just as devastating to a loved one as it is to the patient. Such is the case with Bill, whose wife Gail was diagnosed with lung cancer from exposure to radon four years earlier.

Bill used the Serenity Prayer daily to preserve his sanity as Gail went through surgery and chemotherapy. It seemed that the procedures had done their job until one day when Gail experienced pain in one hip.

Gail and I had met at a presentation just two weeks earlier, when she picked up a card about the *The Only Little Prayer You Need*. "It seemed so simple," she says. "That's what drew me to it." When she learned that the hip pain was a recurrence of cancer, Gail started using the prayer—and so did Bill.

"I spend quite a bit of time walking," Bill tells me. "I find myself repeating the prayer in rhythm to my walking instead of fussing about what's going on with Gail. I find that all those fears melt away."

Bill likes the fact that the prayer is short and easy to remember, and he has added his own wording: "All is going to be well. I place my faith in God. I am not alone. God is with me."

The prayer helps not only while Bill is walking, but also in the middle of the night when he wakes up and starts to think about the cancer. "It helps me get that stuff out of my head," he says.

The calming effect lasts. And he has found comfort in the particular language of the prayer. "The 'fear-based thoughts' wording has helped a lot. Fears don't seem as real to me because they are just thoughts. It takes the power of fear away."

Bill and Gail have had good news of late, as there have been no more recurrences following a round of radiation. For Gail's part, she practices staying in the moment rather than wondering about the future. "The real *f* word in our world is 'fear,'" she says. "The more I read about wellness and cancer, I see that fear plays a tremendous part. Everything changes when it's not there. If we stay in the now, there really isn't so much to be afraid of, is there?"

> If you're dealing with concern over your own health or that of loved ones, ask for this: *Please heal my fear-based thoughts about physical well-being so I can be a calm and healing presence for myself and others.*

LAURA HAS A STORY that probably every parent can relate to. How do you allow for independence and growth when you want to control the fate of the people you love the most?

For Laura, this applies not only to her relationship with her children, but also to her sister's boys, whom she adopted. And it applies to her sister, too, who has long struggled with drug addiction and moved in with Laura when she was released from prison.

"I was the oldest child, and our mom was absent," Laura says, "so I've always been in this role of being the boss. Sometimes I've either passively or passive-aggressively said, 'Let me run the show.' For me, fear and control have gone hand in hand. If there's something I'm afraid of, I'm going to grab onto control harder than ever."

That, she says, is why she's had such a hard time allowing her sister to take on more responsibility and make her own decisions.

"She came to my house directly from prison," Laura tells me. "She was very humble and had the attitude of 'You're the boss of me.' That worked out fine, because I wanted her to do what I said, treating her like a child."

There's no question that Laura's concerns are real. Her sister sometimes forgets to take her medications, and she's gotten behind the wheel when she's not in a state of mind to drive. But Laura's continual efforts to control her sister's behavior keeps both of them stuck.

"I've kept her dependent out of fear that she's going to make bad choices. I've ended up resenting it, and she resents it as well. That doesn't allow for any growth, and I've become a tyrant. I have to just let go and stop being so fearful and let God help her navigate."

The prayer has helped Laura understand that, by making different choices for herself as a parent and sister, she changes the dynamics in those relationships for the better.

"If you cling so tightly to control of the people around you and don't give it up to God, it's going to blow up in your face. I've experienced that enough times to know. But those old habits are hard to break. Until I went to *The Only Little Prayer* workshop, I didn't understand why. It's because fear is such a powerful driver of those habits."

To help change those habits, Laura is making small but significant changes. She took her sister out for an evening of karaoke because her sister loves to sing. "I want us to do more joyful things together," Laura says. She's also relaxing her tendency to judge, so she can meet her sister with "ease rather than animosity" whenever she walks in the room.

Ultimately, Laura now realizes that the best thing she can do as a parent and sister is to ask for her own fear-based thoughts to be healed.

"It seems self-centered that I should focus on me," she says. "But the reality is, if I don't take care of my own spirit, I have no business helping other people."

If your concern for others takes the form of control, **ask for this**: *Please heal my fear-based thoughts about the people in my life so I can treat them with respect and trust God to help them grow.*

# eleven

# How the Prayer Can Change the World

Twice in my life I've had dreams in which I've felt complete bliss. In one dream, which I had when I was seven or eight, my family was in our old DeSoto, driving up the craggy switchbacks of a mountain. When we got to the top, I stepped out of the car and over the top of the mountain, where I saw nothing but verdant green grass. I sat down in the meadow and stared at the green and felt complete peace, the peace that passeth understanding.

In the second dream, I was sent into space in a rocket because God was unhappy with the direction the world was going and wanted to recalibrate it. He planned to stop it for twenty minutes to make the adjustment. During that time, I felt absolute stillness, knowing that no oceans were ebbing and flowing, no clouds were floating. Just sublime stillness and peace.

In both cases, waking up from the dream was a shock and a disappointment. Why couldn't we come close to that sense of peace here in our earthly lives?

For years I tried to figure out what that peace was. But it wasn't until I started studying *A Course in Miracles* that I realized: that peace was the complete absence of fear. It was the feeling of true, pure, untarnished love, the light that shines in all of us, free of any fear-based thoughts or beliefs.

So I still ask the question: Is it possible to experience that peace on earth? I'm not sure, but I think it's worth asking for. And if anything can do it, I believe this prayer may be the key.

Over the centuries, people have asked how we can heal ourselves and the world. How can we stop being violent people? How can we accept one another? How can we share the bounty of the world with everyone? How can we find peace on earth?

The first step is to acknowledge that all the global problems, just like the ones we experience in our individual lives, come from fear. We're stuck in the same spin cycle of despair on both a personal and a universal level because we keep thinking we can get ourselves out of the mess we're in.

But no trying, proving, accomplishing, doing, testing, succeeding, remodeling, accumulating, protesting, attaining, running, or designing will eliminate our fears. Our ego will still be right there, ready to replace one fear with another.

When we ask for our fear-based thoughts to be healed, we're asking to be free of anything that stands in the way of the love of God. I believe this is the meaning of being in this world but not of it: aligning ourselves so consciously and intentionally with our true Self that fear has less and less of a hold on us. It's lovingly quieting the two-year-old and singing her a lullaby.

At a recent women's spirituality workshop, we launched a year of exploring the question, "Are you as happy as you want to be?" We asked the participants to journal about what happiness means to them. Several balked at the word "happy" because it seemed frivolous or superficial. Some preferred words like "contented," "peaceful," "joyful."

But when we started talking about what those words mean, we came to some agreement. Freedom. Forgiveness. Fulfillment. Happiness doesn't necessarily mean that you'll be skipping for joy, but it does mean you'll have peace of mind—the peace of knowing you're safe, taken care of, that you can trust in what surrounds you. I think about it as the peace of Home.

This inner peace is a universal desire because it reflects who we are at our core as children of God. No matter what your religion or culture, inner peace is as coveted as harmony in the home, good health, education, personal freedom, compassion, and a sense of belonging. It is the key to peace on earth, one individual at a time.

So, can the prayer truly help with the most pressing large-scale problems on this planet? Can it really address extreme oppression, violence, poverty, prejudice, famine, disease, corruption, and environmental change?

Let me ask you this: If this prayer can't change it, what can? The big problems we face today are the same ones we've faced for generations, and they all come from deeply ingrained patterns of anger, blame, guilt, and judgment. To build a better world—to finally move forward in a different and significant way—all our thoughts, words, and actions matter. We can only build a world that's different from the one we've built before if those thoughts, words, and actions are powered by love rather than fear.

# Imagine

anyone on the planet who is experiencing domestic violence using this prayer and being healed of their feelings of unworthiness, which they express as victimhood.

# Imagine

the perpetrators of domestic violence using this prayer and being healed of *their* feelings of unworthiness, which they express by exerting dominance over others.

# Imagine

people who have lost their home in a natural disaster using the prayer and finding even greater inner strength to join together and build anew.

# Imagine

people in areas lacking steady employment and sufficient basic services using the prayer and finding new opportunities opening up to support them.

# Imagine

those who stand in the way of education—particularly for girls—using the prayer and feeling less threatened by the empowerment of others.

# Imagine

people engaged in long-standing battles using the prayer and being healed of resentment, clearing a path toward a future forged by forgiveness.

Certainly this may seem idealistic, but that's how we change. We turn toward a higher ideal and make it our destination. We ask for help to, as *A Course in Miracles* says, live "above the battlefield" of chaos and despair. We say a prayer that can boost humanitarian efforts beyond what our human hands can do.

When we see the world through the lens of the prayer, we realize that the destructive force in the world isn't people, it's fear. As long as we view human beings as destructive, we will continue to blame, perpetuating the endless pattern of attack and defense. But when we ask for fear to be healed, we change the conversation. We get to the root cause of violence, poverty, terrorism, apathy, cynicism, and divisiveness. We free ourselves and others to be motived by loving action instead.

*A Course in Miracles* talks about the fact that there's no hierarchy of miracles, and that the energy of fear is the same whether it's one person or one billion. In other words, the shame, guilt, anger, scarcity, and worry we feel on an individual level is the same as those emotions on a global scale. We can't think our way out of them, although every second provides us a fresh opportunity to choose love.

"The healing
has to come
from a different
place, not from our
minds."

The healing has to come from a different place, not from our minds. The *Course* says that our ego mind is rooted in fear and finds it everywhere it looks. This is why you can have what looks like the perfect life and still be miserable, because you're still identifying with the ego.

But the ego's not all we've got. We've also got a connection to the divine, to Creator, Spirit. Love is the other part of us that we can rely on because it connects us to the mind of a higher power.

This shifts our desire from material things or a new job or relationship—what we think will make us happy—to peace of mind, which is the *only* thing that can make us happy. It resets our priorities. And imagine what would happen if we did that on a large scale?

As you say this prayer consistently, you'll be creating peace in your own mind that will emanate from you, transforming your relationships, your work, touching everyone around you. In essence, you'll be creating a ring of peace that will go with you everywhere. This is what makes this practice revolutionary, because the prayer not only heals us, it heals the world.

Imagine if 1,000 people created a ring of peace, or 10,000 people, or 1 million people. At some point—the tipping point—we can create a world that is run less by fear and more by love.

The first step is to become aware of our
fear-based thoughts.

The second step is to say the prayer.

The third step is to witness the miracle and
give thanks for it.

You may want to make a personal commitment that goes something like this: "I commit to using the power of this prayer for the good of myself, those in my life and the world."

Collectively we've created a society of fear—we literally exist in a world of hurt. But by using the prayer, you have the power to put the world in the hands of the Holy Spirit, who can transform it. Fear separates and divides. Love unifies and extends.

When you use the prayer, you help tip the balance toward love.

*twelve*

# Q & A

As you start using the prayer, questions may come to mind. Here are FAQs for quick reference.

Q. What if you don't believe in the Holy Spirit?

A. That's okay. It's not necessary to believe. The only thing that's necessary is the willingness to say the prayer and then witness what happens. As long as there's an opening—even if the aperture is minute—healing will take place.

Q. What if you forget to ask?

A. That's okay, too. You're not being graded on this. And once you remember to ask, one prayer can release you from years' worth of fear.

Q. What is the power I'm invoking?

A. The sacred and all-encompassing power of love.

"It's not necessary to believe. The only thing that's necessary is the willingness to say the prayer and then witness what happens."

Q. What if the prayer doesn't seem to be working?

A. Keep doing it anyway. You have years' worth of fear instilled in you, so it can take a while before you start to feel any shift. On the other hand, you may feel a change immediately.

Q. What should I do after saying the prayer?

A. Pay attention. Start noticing how you feel and how the world around you changes. You'll probably experience more of what we might think of as serendipity, or a sense that events in your day are flowing easily and smoothly, like someone is choreographing them for you. In essence, that's exactly what's happening. You are experiencing the natural order of the universe, unimpeded by your barriers of worry and control. Relax into it. Allow yourself to be carried along.

Q. What will I experience over time?

A. More peace of mind. A sense that things will be okay without your needing to worry or stress over them.

Q. Will this make me lazy or unambitious?

A. Not unless you want it to. Experiencing the ease of life when your fears are healed makes it possible to see the beauty around you and to contribute in ways you may not have thought of before. It makes it possible for you to do what makes you happy, what you came here to do, rather than trying to shoehorn your life into someone else's expectations.

Q. Will all the problems and challenges in my life go away?

A. Not necessarily, but you will experience them differently. You may view them with grace and forgiveness rather than anger and resentment. You will replace blame with understanding. You will no longer need to create or perpetuate drama in your life. As issues come up, you'll be free to make thoughtful decisions for the good of all. You will stop trying to please others at your own expense. And you'll be healed of the need for a pattern of attack and self-defense, in your own mind and in the outer world.

"Ask for your expectations and impatience to be healed, because they're both forms of fear."

**Q.** I'm getting annoyed by asking over and over and not seeing results. What do I do?

**A.** Ask for your expectations and impatience to be healed, because they're both forms of fear.

**Q.** I'm asking for my world to change, and the people who annoy me are still here. What am I doing wrong?

**A.** The key is that you don't ask for different circumstances or different people in your life, you ask for *yourself* to be changed. When that occurs, the circumstances and people in your life will shift.

**Q.** Can I use the prayer on someone else's behalf?

**A.** Yes, although the intent is not to "fix" that person to please you. One woman used the prayer on behalf of a young man with severe attachment disorder whose whole life, she says, is ruled by fear. Over a period of about three months, she saw him starting to trust more—a change she calls "truly amazing."

Q. I've been using the prayer for several days, and today I feel panicked over things that haven't bothered me before. Why is that?

A. The healing is going deeper. The ego is getting nervous and is acting out. Keep asking for *all* your fear-based thinking to be healed at the deepest levels.

Q. Should I ask for specific thoughts to be healed, or thoughts in general? For instance, is it better to ask for all my fears about money to be healed, or should I ask for my fear about retirement savings to be healed?

A. Both are equally powerful prayers. You can alternate, or just ask for whatever is on your mind at any moment. Have no fear: you can't make a mistake.

"Keep asking for *all* your fear-based thinking to be healed at the deepest levels."

*thirteen*

# And Finally . . .

You know how it goes. You think, *If I can just get past this, then life will be good.* Then, the moment that challenge is out of the way, what happens? Another comes to take its place.

I know what it's like to live my life on that runaway train. One day I'm nervous about a deadline. Then I meet the deadline, everyone's happy with my work, and I'm immediately anxious about money . . . or a conversation I need to have . . . or a hundred other things that are waiting in the wings to keep me in a constant state of anxiety.

In truth, I have a wonderful life. A loving husband, truly wonderful friends and family, a beautiful home, work I enjoy, good health. And yet, when I started really paying attention to my thoughts after CR-V day, I realized that I've been constantly drugged by fear. I think most of us are.

No wonder we're tired, cranky, short-tempered, or difficult to get along with. Or, worse, violent, calculating, unforgiving. It's because we live in fear and don't even know it. Or if we do, we don't know how to get out of it.

So here's the answer:

Say the prayer.

Say the prayer.
Say the prayer.
All day long, say the prayer.

# *Please*

# heal

# *my*

# *fear-based*

# THOUGHTS.

In May 2004, a story in *Smithsonian* magazine documented the Dalai Lama's recent visit to the United States. Before he arrived, researchers at the Massachusetts Institute of Technology (MIT) decided to study him and find out why he was so darn happy all the time. Clearly, they thought, there must be something wrong.

Embedded in the article is a fascinating statistic. It seems that, in a survey of thirty years of psychology publications, researchers counted 46,000 papers on depression—and 400 on joy.

Those numbers suggest a sacred truth: we get what we look for. If we've looked for depression 46,000 times and joy only 400, it says a lot about what we're focused on and what we want to find.

We're starting with the premise that life is a struggle and we have to fix it. But this is the fear-based ego trying to make a case for its existence. It looks for evidence every day that this world is a sick and dangerous place. And, of course, if that's what you're looking for, you don't have to look far to find it.

But what if we started with a different premise? What if we began with the belief that, as children of God, our

"This is not about positive thinking. It's about being free from the fear-based ego."

natural state is one of balance, harmony, and well-being? What if there were 46,000 articles on joy and only 400 on depression? People would say we're ignoring the problem or living in denial. But *A Course in Miracles*, along with other spiritual texts, says that balance and harmony *are* our natural inheritance as children of God. This is not about positive thinking. It's about being free from the fear-based ego. We simply cannot move forward while we're in the negative spin cycle of fear-based thoughts.

*A Course in Miracles* says that love is real and fear is not. But fear can seem mighty real when you're carrying it around like an elephant on your back all day. When it fills up your cells and gives you a nervous stomach or headaches or heart problems or cancer. When it interferes with your ability to sleep, to have happy relationships, to pursue your dreams.

In light of how scary the world often seems, we may think we need to be fearless. But the prayer creates a new definition of that word. Instead of being brave in the face of danger, it means experiencing greater peace of mind. Every time you say the prayer, you become more fear-less.

The prayer shifts our focus from the outside world to our inner connection with our true Self and God. When you ask the Holy Spirit to heal your fear-based thoughts, you acknowledge that your happiness doesn't depend on the chaotic world around you. Instead, it depends on the steadfast peace of God within you.

I believe our commitment to the healing of fear is the key to the next step in spiritual evolution. To bring about great change on this planet, we need to collaborate with Spirit on an individual level. In the past, this has been inhibited by teachings that only spiritual or religious leaders have a direct line to God. But in the past few decades, we've returned to an understanding that, as children of God, we are *all* connected directly to Spirit, and we can develop that relationship in community *and* in the privacy of our own contemplation.

If we are to truly create a different world for ourselves and others, we need to work with powers beyond our own hands. But when we're governed by fear, that collaboration is crippled or, at best, slowed. Trying to arrive at a different destination using our egos as vehicles is like trying to paddle around the world in a canoe.

To work as co-creators and partners with the Divine, we need to be free to give and receive direct communication without the interfering static of fear. Just think of the woman who, on saying the prayer the first time, heard the words, "FINALLY! Now we can really get some things done!" I believe that exuberant message is for all of us. Spirit is eager to heal our fears—not just because we'll experience the abundance and joy of life, but because we'll be better able to bring about positive changes, helping to shift the dynamics of the planet.

We all have an infinite loop of old tapes playing in our minds just like the anger and frustration I felt on CR-V day. I asked to let go of those tapes, I tried to ignore them, I attempted to understand them, I tried to shift my thoughts to something else. But until the prayer showed up, those thoughts were stuck on "play."

Since CR-V day, I've seen that the prayer not only erases the tapes, it truly can help you experience everything you want in life: abundance, health, vitality, love, and peace of mind.

"Healing of fear is
the key to the next
step in spiritual
evolution."

Many things have shifted in my life in the months since I've been saying the prayer, but the overarching change is an ever-expanding capacity for joy. Fear no longer limits how much room there is for love in my life.

The ego, though, doesn't want you to heal. It's invested in keeping you stuck and unhappy, so it will shut you down and make you forget to do the simplest thing in the world: Say six words in your heart and mind that can change your life experience and make you feel free, happy and light. If you need to, write down the prayer and carry it with you, put it on your phone, do something to remind yourself of it until it becomes routine.

It took time to get where you are, so you have to give the prayer time and patience. This can be difficult some days when you find yourself constantly asking. You start to realize how relentless the negative and fear-based thoughts really are. And it can seem overwhelming, as though you're staring down an advancing army. How can you ever win? That's when you remember, *you* can't, but the Holy Spirit can.

Our two-year-old egos are not capable of being self-aware, or self-correcting enough to let go of the fear. We have to ask a power greater than ourselves to lift that burden from us—to truly change our minds, to bring us to right-mindedness. This is the real meaning of righteous thinking . . . to be aligned with the energy of love.

So keep asking. Be vigilant. This is spiritual practice. One request to heal your thoughts is not going to take care of everything. Be mindful. Practice this more than anything you've practiced in your whole life. But you won't be practicing in vain, even if at times it feels that way. The rattles in your dashboard will start to go away, and many more may disappear completely.

Using the prayer is not about never having another fear-based thought. This world is filled with them. Our minds are filled with them. But you can shift the balance. You can reach the point where you wake up in the morning and go to bed at night satisfied and content rather than stressed and fitful. You can experience a life in which your relationships are harmonious and you feel supported and loved. You can find purpose in your work and balance your profession with pursuits that bring you joy. You can remove the barriers to abundance and well-being. You can show your kids the beauty of this world and see the light of God in the people you meet.

It's all possible. And it's what you deserve. It's what everyone deserves.

So say the prayer. It takes only a second. It's the simplest thing in the world. And results are 100 percent guaranteed.

A good trade-off, I'd say, for saying six little words.

*Please*

# heal

*my*

*fear-based*

T H O U G H T S .

# Acknowledgments

From the day the prayer showed up in my life, this project has had a momentum and power all its own. I have no doubt that the prayer was meant to be shared, and that unseen hands guided it to a loving and dedicated team.

My greatest thanks go to . . .

My agent, Stephany Evans of FinePrint Literary Management, for immediately recognizing the power of the prayer and unfailingly offering her expert advice and friendship along the way.

My editor, Caroline Pincus, for championing this book from the beginning and giving it her thoughtful and thorough attention. She has been an invaluable resource and steward.

The design staff at Red Wheel/Weiser for treating the manuscript with great care and craftsmanship, exceeding my vision of what it could be 100 times over.

Claire Elizabeth Terry, who made miracles happen by contacting leaders around the world on behalf of the prayer. She has become a treasured friend through this process.

My *A Course in Miracles* students for their patience as I talked ceaselessly about fear-based and love-based thoughts, and for their constant encouragement.

All those, named and unnamed, who allowed me to tell their stories in the book. I'm inspired by the depth of their wisdom and faith.

My husband, Bob, for always being willing to listen when I say, "I have something to tell you"—even when it's about rattles in the dashboard appearing (and disappearing). His steadfastness, and his ability to question and support, remind me every day of the gifts we're meant to offer one another.

The one Spirit who comforted me with the prayer in the first place and makes everything possible. I can't express the depth of my gratitude and awe.

And to all those who use this prayer and share it with others. Thank you for helping to shift this world from fear to love.

# About the Author

Photo by Amy Allen

Debra Landwehr Engle is co-founder of a women's program of personal and spiritual growth and teaches classes in A Course in Miracles. She is the author of *Grace from the Garden: Changing the World One Garden at a Time* and has contributed essays to international collections, including *The Art of Living: A Practical Guide to Being Alive*.

Widely traveled as a speaker and workshop facilitator, she lives with her husband Bob in Madison County, Iowa, home of the famed covered bridges.

You can visit her at *www.debraengle.com*.

Hampton Roads Publishing Company

... for the evolving human spirit

Hampton Roads Publishing Company publishes books on a variety of subjects, including spirituality, health, and other related topics.

For a copy of our latest trade catalog, call (978) 465-0504 or visit our distributor's website at *www.redwheelweiser.com*. You can also sign up for our newsletter and special offers by going to *www.redwheelweiser.com/newsletter/*.